STRIPS & STRINGS

16 Sparkling Quilts

EVELYN SLOPPY

Martingale™
& COMPANY

Martingale™
& COMPANY

That Patchwork Place®

That Patchwork Place® is an imprint of
Martingale & Company™.

Strips and Strings: 16 Sparkling Quilts
© 2003 by Evelyn Sloppy

Martingale & Company
20205 144th Avenue NE
Woodinville, WA 98072-8478 USA
www.martingale-pub.com

Printed in China

08 07 06 05 04 03   8 7 6 5 4 3 2 1

Credits

President — Nancy J. Martin

CEO — Daniel J. Martin

Publisher — Jane Hamada

Editorial Director — Mary V. Green

Managing Editor — Tina Cook

Technical Editor — Laurie Baker

Copy Editor — Liz McGehee

Design Director — Stan Green

Illustrator — Laurel Strand

Cover and
Text Designer — Shelly Garrison

Photographer — Brent Kane

Mission Statement

We are dedicated to providing quality products and service by working together to inspire creativity and to enrich the lives we touch.

Library of Congress Cataloging-in-Publication Data
Sloppy, Evelyn
    Strips and strings : 16 sparkling quilts / Evelyn Sloppy.
        p. cm.
    ISBN 1-56477-466-X
    1. Patchwork—Patterns. 2. Strip quilting.
    3. Crazy quilts. I. Title.
    TT835 .S5547 2003
    746.46'041—dc21
                                        2002152795

Dedication

To my mother, Winifred DeGering, who tried to teach me to be frugal and not to waste a thing. However, I am quite the opposite, spending money on the things I love and throwing away anything I don't have an immediate need for—except when it comes to quilting. Then I save the smallest scraps, thinking I might later use them in another quilt, and I never throw away a magazine or book that might give me an idea in the future. So, Mom, your teaching did take hold in some small way. My "string quilts" will always remind me of you. Thank you for being proud of me. I will always love you.

Acknowledgments

My sincere thanks go to:

My friend Jeannie Brewster, who so willingly shares everything she knows about machine quilting with me and so beautifully quilted "Tranquil Treasures";

My niece Heather Willoughby, who shared her artistic talents by drawing the bunnies for "Bunny Love";

Laurie Baker, Mary Green, Karen Soltys, Terry Martin, and the entire staff of Martingale & Company for all the hard work involved in putting *Strips & Strings* together;

And especially, my husband, Dean, who has been so patient while I've written three books in the past year, never complaining about the lack of home-cooked meals or the absence of my company. He's a real jewel.

Contents

INTRODUCTION — 6

QUILTMAKING BASICS — 7

ASSEMBLY AND FINISHING — 16

PROJECTS

    PLAID OBSESSION — 21

    BABY FINGERS — 26

    COUNTRY MANOR CHARM — 29

    STARSTRUCK — 34

    AUTUMN SPLENDOR — 36

    VISIONS OF FABRICS PAST — 40

    ANGEL KISSES — 44

    IT'S A BLUE SKY DAY — 49

    WINTER WISHES — 55

    BUNNY LOVE — 60

    ON THE WILD SIDE — 67

    THE ELEGANCE OF RED — 73

    STARS OF FREEDOM — 79

    DAZZLING DIAMONDS — 82

    TRANQUIL TREASURES — 86

    RAINY DAY BLUES — 91

ABOUT THE AUTHOR — 96

Introduction

My love for scrappy quilts and my need to avoid waste has led me to save leftover fabric from the quilts I make. When I first started quilting, I saved all these scraps in a small plastic container. As my obsession with quilting overtook me, so did my scraps. So, I separated my scraps by color and used several containers to hold them. Soon, the containers were overflowing, so I had to advance to larger containers. One day, I decided I must make a quilt using just these scraps. This quilt would be "free," since the fabric had been purchased and used for other quilts. I painstakingly cut out 2" and 4" squares from my scraps and put together a beautiful queen-size quilt. However, I could not see spending the time it had taken to make too many more the same way.

I like intricate and complicated-looking quilts, and I also like strip-piecing and shortcut methods. So, I took a closer look at the string-pieced quilts I had seen. Traditionally, string quilts were pieced from narrow strips of leftover fabric. Generally, these strips were sewn onto a paper or fabric foundation with no regard to color coordination, so many of them are very busy looking. But, they were made for utilitarian purposes rather than beauty, and thrifty quilt-makers enjoyed using all their scraps for these "free" quilts.

I loved the idea of having so many fabrics in one quilt and using more of my scraps in a shorter time. So, I set about making a string-pieced quilt on a muslin foundation. Following the ones I had seen, I used strips of varying widths from an assortment of my scraps, with no regard to color or value. This was difficult for me, as I had always enjoyed picking out the perfect fabrics for my projects. As I pieced and watched my pile of scraps shrink, I wasn't sure how this multitude of clashing fabrics could ever become a quilt I could

be proud of. And, sure enough, it wasn't. I just couldn't accept the spontaneity of all those fabrics together. I tried overdyeing the quilt, hoping to unify the fabrics a bit. It did help somewhat, but not enough.

Not one to give up on an idea, I decided spontaneity just did not work for me. I could still make string quilts but make them more coordinated. If I didn't have enough scraps of the colors I was using, I could add to them from my stash. I wanted my string quilts to be just as stunning as the quilts for which I purchase special fabrics. Also, my string quilts would not have to be completely string pieced. Substituting just a portion of a block with string piecing would give it more depth, texture, and interest than if I used just one fabric. And last, to make the quilts less time-consuming, I decided to sew the strips together into larger units and then cut out the pieces I needed from these units. This would be faster than sewing each little piece onto a foundation.

Combining my love of scrappy quilts and traditional blocks, I set about designing the string-pieced quilts for this book. Everything I saw, I wanted to modify for string piecing. I found the way to keep these quilts from looking too busy was to stick with a specific color family (or families) or theme. I also found that I could unify the quilt by using just one fabric for the background.

Although all of the quilts in this book are quite simple, easy enough for the beginning quilter, some may look rather advanced. Do not be fooled. They can all be put together rather easily using the techniques I've developed.

After making all of these quilts, my scrap bins are definitely lighter, but still not empty. Now I can buy more fabric with less guilt! I hope you enjoy making these quilts as much as I have.

Quiltmaking Basics

Fabric Selection

Select high-quality, 100% cotton fabrics. They hold their shape well and are easy to handle. Don't feel that you have to have a lot of scraps. Even beginning quilters who probably don't have a large accumulation of scraps can make these string-pieced quilts. Here are my suggestions for acquiring scraps for string quilts.

- Use leftover fabric pieces from previous quilting, crafting, or clothing projects.

- Cut strips from discarded or outgrown items of clothing.

- Purchase fat quarters (18" x 21" pieces of fabric) or fat eighths (9" x 21" pieces of fabric).

- Look for scrap bags that many quilt shops put together from their own leftovers. These usually contain small pieces of many fabrics and are packaged at bargain prices. I snatch these up whenever I find them.

- Cut a strip or two from your larger yardage pieces.

- Arrange for a swap with your quilting friends. If six people each bring ten fat quarters that have been cut into 3" strips, you could go home with 3" strips of sixty different fabrics!

- Let your friends and neighbors know that you are accepting donations of cotton fabrics. Once word gets out, you could be swamped by the boxes of fabric you receive.

- Have a "guilt sale" at your quilt guild. Ask members to bring fabrics they are no longer interested in using and mark them at bargain prices. One person's trash could be another's treasure. Donate the money raised to your guild for future charitable projects.

- If you belong to a quilting group that gets together and sews, check out what the others throw away. I save anything at least 3" square or strips at least 1" x 4". Your friends will be glad that someone will be using their discards and will start saving all their pieces for you.

Once you start accumulating a collection of scraps, you must effectively organize them. I started out using shoe boxes but quickly advanced to lidded plastic containers in various sizes. These can be labeled and stored under beds, in closets, on open shelves, or even in a pantry. (After all, you don't have much time for cooking once you get hooked on quilting.) Just don't forget where you have stored these, and dig into them often for your quilting projects. When I get ready to start a new scrap quilt, I always check my scrap bins once I've decided on a color recipe or theme for the quilt. I may find just a piece or two to use, but quite often I will find many more.

As I clean up my sewing room after finishing a quilt, I sort all the leftover pieces of fabric. Pieces that are fat eighths or larger go back on my shelves; anything smaller is put into the appropriate scrap bin. I separate my scraps by color or theme. I use separate containers for reds, blues, greens, browns and neutrals, yellows, purples, multicolored, Christmas or holiday, plaids, flannels, children's bright prints, and '30s reproductions. You won't have as large a variety as I have when you first start out collecting, so you might want to separate them into just lights and darks, for example. As your collection grows, examine your stash and make up a new scrap bin for areas where you are accumulating lots of pieces. I buy lots of fat quarters since I love scrappy quilts, and often one fat quarter can find its way into five or six different quilts.

How do you decide on a theme for your string quilt? Go to all the quilt shows you can, read lots of books and magazines, and see what really attracts you. I find that the fabric is usually what draws me to a quilt. Make a mental note of what you particularly like about a quilt. Over time, you will know what color combinations really speak to your heart. String quilts made from multicolored fabrics are very popular, but you may find that you like one-color quilts. You can still make string quilts using this recipe. "Angel Kisses" (page 44) and "Rainy Day Blues" (page 91) use a variety of fabrics in one color. Or, you may prefer pastels to darker Civil War prints. Whatever your choice, you can make a beautiful string-pieced quilt.

My problem is that I love almost every color and want to make one of everything I see. Just let your instincts take over and don't fret that you have no artistic background. I certainly don't, but I have great fun selecting the fabrics for my quilts. Quite often, I will start out with a group of fat quarters that appeal to me and then add to it from my scraps or other fabric pieces. "Dazzling Diamonds" (page 82) started out with a fat-quarter collection. I particularly liked the greens and purples, so I added lots of other scraps with that color theme. By the time I was finished, I really had to hunt for the original fat-quarter prints that had been the inspiration for the quilt. For "Bunny Love" (page 60), the background fabric was my starting point. I pulled out the soft pinks, greens, and yellows from it and didn't even know I was going to appliqué bunnies until I had quite a few blocks pieced. I had originally intended to appliqué flower baskets, but the fabrics said "bunnies" to me. Listen, and the fabrics will speak to you.

Tip

Be sure to use plaids, stripes, large and small prints, and solids for the string-pieced portions of your quilts. The variety will give your project texture and interest.

String piecing a portion of your quilt will take more time than just using one fabric piece, but I think you'll agree the difference is well worth your effort. For instance, you can see how much more interesting the string-pieced blocks from "It's a Blue Sky Day" (page 49) and "Rainy Day Blues" (page 91) are than the traditional blocks. Learn this technique and you can incorporate it into many of the quilts you make. They will come alive with string piecing.

Block from
"Rainy Day Blues"

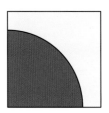

Traditional
Drunkard's Path block

Block from
"It's a Blue Sky Day"

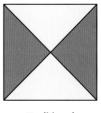

Traditional
Hourglass block

Yardage requirements are based on 42" of usable fabric after preshrinking. For the string-pieced sections of the quilt, which will be indicated in the Materials section for each project, you may buy fat eighths (9" x 21" pieces of fabric), fat quarters (18" x 21" pieces of fabric), or the standard yardage to total the required amount of fabric. Try to use as many fabrics as you can—the more the better. If you are using fabric scraps from your stash and you're not sure you have enough, just start sewing. After a few blocks, you will be able to tell how fast your scraps are shrinking. If you feel you might need more, buy a few more pieces and mix them in with what you have. When you mix up your blocks before you start sewing them together, your quilt will look great.

Do not cut up all the fabric you intend to use before you start piecing the blocks. Just cut enough strips to make a few blocks and then study these blocks. Are you happy with them? Maybe certain fabrics stick out as not being right. If so, pull these fabrics out before you cut them all into strips. This happens often to me, maybe because I don't have a formal art background and have a harder time knowing that something will not work until I try it. On several quilts I had intended to make for this book, I made six or seven blocks and then tossed the whole idea because it just didn't work. I was glad I hadn't spent hours cutting all my strips before I even started piecing!

Preparing Fabric

Make it a habit to prewash your fabrics after you purchase them so that they're ready to sew when you are. Prewashing your fabrics will take care of any shrinkage and will also remove any excess dye. To prewash your fabrics, place all of the fabrics into the washing machine and fill the tub with water. Do not use any detergent. Let the fabrics soak for ten minutes and then run them through the spin cycle to remove the water. This method does not remove the sizing from the fabrics, so they do not ravel and tangle up with each other. Dry the fabrics in the dryer, and then fold them neatly and store them. I do not press my fabrics until I am ready to use them. If you will be working with bias edges, use spray sizing when pressing the fabric so the edges will not stretch out of shape as easily.

Rotary Cutting

Instructions for quick-and-easy rotary cutting are provided wherever possible. All measurements include standard ¼"-wide seam allowances. For those unfamiliar with rotary cutting, a brief introduction is provided below. For more detailed information, see *Shortcuts: A Concise Guide to Rotary Cutting* by Donna Lynn Thomas (Martingale & Company, 1999). Reverse this entire procedure if you are left-handed.

1. Fold the fabric in half lengthwise, matching the selvages. Align the grain lines as much as possible so that the crosswise grain line runs parallel to the cut edge, and the lengthwise grain line runs parallel to the folded edge. Place the folded fabric on the cutting mat with the folded edge closest to you. Align a square ruler, such as a Bias Square®, along the folded edge of the fabric. Butt a long, straight ruler against the left edge of the square ruler, just covering the uneven raw edges along the left side of the fabric as shown.

2. Remove the square ruler and cut along the right edge of the long ruler. Discard the cut strip.

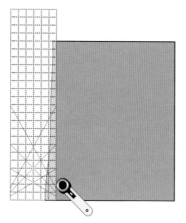

3. To cut strips, align the newly cut edge of the fabric with the appropriate ruler markings. For example, to cut a 3"-wide strip, place the 3" ruler marking at the edge of the fabric.

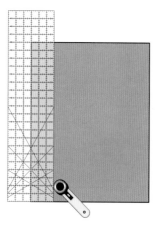

4. To cut squares, cut strips of the required widths. Trim the selvage ends of the strips. Align the left edge of a strip with the desired ruler markings—the length measurement should match the width measurement of the strip. Cut the strip into squares.

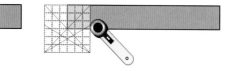

5. To cut rectangles, match the strip width to the shorter side of the desired rectangle. Use the measurement of the longer side when cutting the strip into rectangles. For example, to cut a 3" x 5" rectangle, cut a 3"-wide strip and then cut 5"-long segments from it.

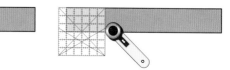

Machine Piecing

The most important thing to remember about machine piecing is the need to maintain a consistent ¼"-wide seam allowance. Otherwise, the quilt blocks will not be the desired finished size. If your quilt blocks finish to the wrong size, the size of everything else in the quilt will be affected, including alternate blocks, sashings, and borders. Measurements for all components of a quilt are based on blocks that finish accurately to the desired size plus ¼" on each edge for seam allowances.

Take the time to establish an exact ¼"-wide seam guide on your machine. Some machines have a special quilting foot that measures exactly ¼" from the center needle position to the edge of the foot. This feature allows you to use the edge of the presser foot to guide the fabric for a perfect ¼"-wide seam allowance.

If your machine doesn't have such a foot, create a seam guide by placing the edge of a piece of tape, moleskin, or a magnetic seam guide ¼" from the needle.

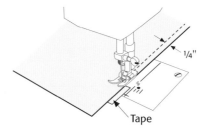

Perform the following test to make sure the method you are using results in an accurate ¼"-wide seam.

1. Cut 3 strips of fabric, 1½" x 3".

2. Sew the long edges of the strips together, using the edge of the presser foot or a seam guide you have made. Press seams toward the outer edges. After sewing and pressing, the center strip should measure exactly 1" wide. If it doesn't, adjust the needle or seam guide in the proper direction.

Tip

I find that I need to take a scant ¼" seam (that is, about two threads less than ¼") in order for my measurements to come out correctly. This is because the pressing takes up a few threads. Try this if your sample strip is too small.

String-Piecing Techniques

String-pieced units are the building blocks of string-pieced quilts. The units are made by sewing various widths of fabric strips, or strings, together along their long edges. Generally, the unfinished widths of the strings can vary from 1" to 2½". The lengths of the strings will vary, depending on the pattern, but they will generally be anywhere from 4" to 22". If you have smaller strings you'd like to use, you can piece them together to achieve the necessary length. You may sew them together in a straight seam, but I prefer a diagonal seam because it is not as visible. Press the seams open.

Join strings with straight or diagonal seam.

Stitch the strings together along the long edges until you have a piece the size indicated in the project instructions or larger. For instance, if you need a unit that is at least 8" long and 8" high, sew strings that are 8" or longer together until you have a piece that is at least 8" wide. This may take anywhere from six to eight strings, depending on the string widths. Although an accurate ¼" seam allowance is desirable, it is not crucial, since you are just sewing to a desired measurement. Use strings of varying widths to make your quilt more interesting. Start and end with strings that are wider; the unit will be trimmed to the exact measurement needed and you don't want these pieces trimmed too small. After sewing the strings together, press the seams in one direction. Place the unit on your cutting mat and trim it to the exact measurement needed.

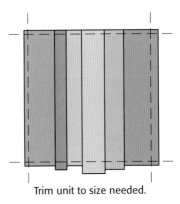

Trim unit to size needed.

If the directions call for shorter lengths of strings but you have longer pieces, you can sew the longer pieces together and then cut the unit into the smaller lengths required. This will save you time. The rule of thumb is to add 1" to the lengths required to allow for trimming. For instance, let's say you need 5" lengths. I would make sure my strings are about 6" before I sew them together and then trim the unit to 5". If I want to make two units at once, I would need 11" strings (5" x 2 + 1"). I could make three units at once by using 16" lengths (5" x 3 + 1"). When I'm working with my scraps, I have lots of different lengths and would like to use them all without cutting them into the smaller sizes. So, for the preceeding example, I would sort my strings into piles of 6+", 11+", and 16+" lengths. I would sew the 6" strings together for one unit; then I would sew the 11" strings together and cut them into two units; the 16" strings would then be sewn together and cut into three units. The instructions for each quilt will generally show the shortest-size lengths you can use, but use longer lengths if you have them, and then cut them into multiple units.

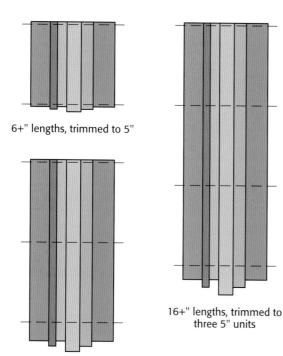

6+" lengths, trimmed to 5"

16+" lengths, trimmed to three 5" units

11+" lengths, trimmed to two 5" units

String-Pieced Units for 60° Triangles

"Stars of Freedom" (page 79) and "Dazzling Diamonds" (page 82) are made up of 60° string-pieced triangles. You will construct the string-pieced units by staggering the ends of the strips rather than having the strip ends even. This will eliminate waste from both ends of the strip and allow you to cut more triangles from the unit. Offset the strips about ½". The measurement does not have to be exact, but if you have a difficult time eyeballing it, cut out a small piece of paper ½" wide by about 3" long.

Use this as a guide when sewing the strings together; it is easier than using a ruler.

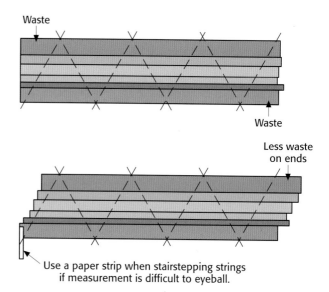

Waste

Waste

Less waste on ends

Use a paper strip when stairstepping strings if measurement is difficult to eyeball.

To cut the triangles, line up the 60°-angle mark on your ruler with the bottom of a string-pieced unit. Cut along the left edge of the ruler. Turn the ruler over and position it so that the 60°-angle mark lines up with the bottom of the unit and the ruler right edge aligns with the upper edge of the previous cut as shown. Cut along the right edge of the ruler. Turn the ruler back over and rotate it so the 60° angle aligns with the top edge of the unit, and the right edge aligns with the lower edge of the previous cut. Cut along the right edge of the ruler. Continue rotating the ruler in this manner to cut the triangles from the string-pieced units.

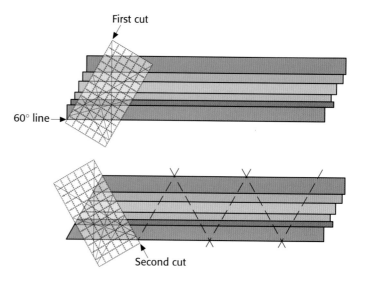

First cut

60° line

Second cut

String-Pieced Units for Bias Squares

This is a quick method for making bias squares. The squares will have bias edges when you are finished, but if you handle them with care, you won't have any problems.

Place a string-pieced unit and a plain strip of the same size right sides together; sew along both long edges.

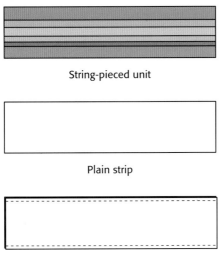

String-pieced unit

Plain strip

Right sides together

Using a square ruler, align the unfinished measurement of the bias-square size needed with the bottom seam line, and cut along both sides of the ruler. Rotate the ruler, line up the measurements with the top seam line, and cut along both sides of the ruler. Continue to the end of the strips. It may be easier for you to rotate the strips rather than the ruler.

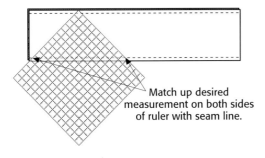

Match up desired measurement on both sides of ruler with seam line.

Remove any stitches at the point of each block. Open up your block and press the center seam in one direction. The blocks will be the exact measurement that you need. No trimming is necessary.

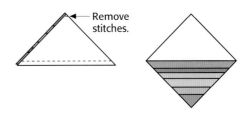

Remove stitches.

By substituting the plain strip with a pieced strip (not a string-pieced strip), we can obtain various other units, but the method is exactly the same.

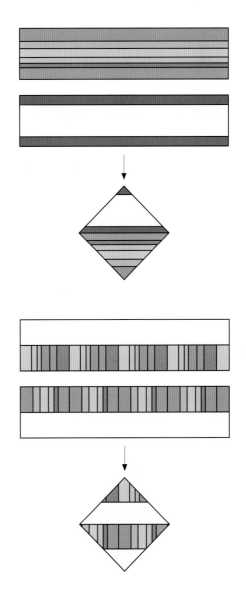

To make a bias square that is entirely string pieced, make 2 string-pieced units, staggering one strip to the left and the other to the right. The strings should be offset by about 1". Trim each unit to the required width.

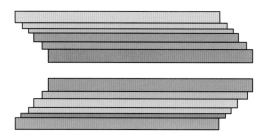

Place the two units right sides together and sew along both long edges.

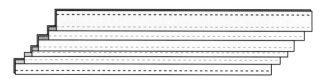

Cut out the squares, using the same method as used previously for the string-pieced unit and plain unit. Remove the stitches at the point of each block, and press the center seam in one direction.

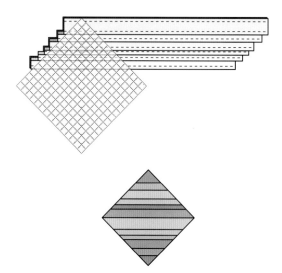

No-Math Method for Determining Size of String-Pieced Units

If you want to substitute a plain square for a bias-square string-pieced unit in any quilt you are making, use my quick, no-math method to determine the height of the units you need to start with. Let's say you want to make a 6" finished square. Add 1" to this measurement (6" + 1" = 7"). Place a ruler on the 45° line of your cutting mat and go to the 7" mark on the ruler. The measurement on the cutting mat at that point is the height you need to make the units. The 7" mark puts us at the 5" height measurement. For each square, make 2 units, each 5" high, sew them together along the long edge, and then cut the square to 6½" for a 6" finished square.

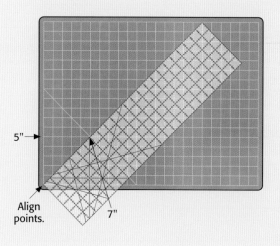

5" →

Align points.

7"

Fusible-Web Appliqué

The appliquéd motifs for "Angel Kisses" (page 44) and "Bunny Love" (page 60) were applied to the background fabric with fusible web. This quick method secures the appliqués to the fabric and does not technically require any additional treatment. However, I prefer to add a buttonhole stitch around the edges of each shape for additional security and a neater finish. Because fusible web can add thickness to your appliqué, making it difficult to stitch through, choose a lightweight fusible product for your projects. Always follow the manufacturer's directions for the fusible-web product you select.

When using fusible web for appliqué, the appliqué patterns must be the reverse image of how they will appear on the quilt. The patterns in this book already have been reversed. Do not reverse the patterns and do not add seam allowances to them unless you intend to hand appliqué. If you prefer hand-appliqué methods, you will need to reverse the appliqué patterns and add turn-under allowances.

Follow these steps to make the appliqués for the projects in this book:

1. Follow the project directions to trace the indicated appliqué patterns onto the paper side of the fusible web. Leave a small amount of space between each shape.

2. Cut out the traced shapes, leaving a ⅛" margin. Following the manufacturer's directions, fuse the appliqué shapes to the wrong side of the appropriate fabrics.

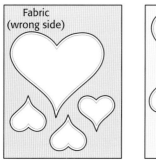
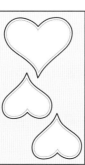

Fabric
(wrong side)

Tip

To reduce the stiffening caused by some fusible-web products, I cut out the center part of the fusible-web motif before I apply it to the fabric.

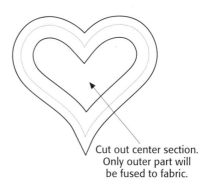

Cut out center section.
Only outer part will
be fused to fabric.

3. Once the fabric is cool, cut out the shapes on the drawn line. Gently peel away the paper backing from the fabric. Position the appliqué pieces on the background as indicated for each project and fuse them in place.

4. After all of the appliqués have been fused in place, buttonhole stitch around each shape. I prefer to use No. 8 pearl cotton to buttonhole stitch, but you can also use two strands of embroidery floss. To make the buttonhole stitch, bring the needle up from the wrong side of the background fabric at A, just off the edge of the appliqué piece. Insert the needle back down through the fabric at B, inside the appliqué piece, and back up at C, just off the edge of the appliqué piece and over the thread. Repeat, keeping the stitches an even distance apart and the same distance into the appliqué piece. You may also appliqué pieces by machine. Consult your owner's manual.

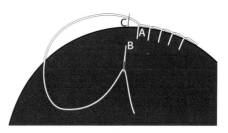

Assembly and Finishing

Now that you've finished the blocks for your quilt, you're ready to sew them together and add borders, if desired. The blocks will be sewn together in either a straight or diagonal setting. Sometimes sashing is added between the blocks. Borders may be either straight or mitered.

Assembling Straight-Set Quilts

1. Arrange the blocks as indicated in the directions for each quilt project.

2. Sew the blocks together in horizontal rows; press the seams in opposite directions from row to row.

3. Sew the rows together, making sure to match the seams between the blocks.

Assembling Diagonally Set Quilts

1. Arrange the blocks and side setting triangles as shown for each quilt project.

2. Sew the blocks together in diagonal rows; press the seams in opposite directions from row to row.

3. Sew the rows together, making sure to match the seams between the blocks. Sew the corner setting triangles to the quilt top last.

Adding Borders

For best results, do not cut border strips and sew them directly to the quilt sides without measuring first. Because the edges of a quilt often measure slightly longer than the distance through the quilt center due to stretching during construction, measure the quilt top through the center in both directions to determine how long to cut the border strips. This step ensures that the finished quilt will be as straight and as "square" as possible, without wavy edges.

Plain border strips are commonly cut along the crosswise grain and seamed where extra length is needed. Borders cut from the lengthwise grain of fabric require extra yardage, but seaming the required length is then unnecessary. Borders cut from the lengthwise grain also have less stretch than borders cut from the crosswise grain and will be less likely to have wavy edges. You may add borders that have straight-cut corners or mitered corners.

Straight-Cut Borders

1. Measure the length of the quilt top through the center. Cut two border strips to this measurement, piecing as necessary; mark the center of the quilt edges and the border strips. With right sides together, pin the borders to the sides of the quilt top, matching the center marks and ends and easing as necessary. Sew the border strips in place. Press the seams toward the border strips.

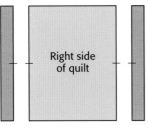

Mark centers.

2. Measure the width of the quilt top through the center, including the side borders just added. Cut two border strips to this measurement, piecing as necessary; mark the center of the quilt edges and the border strips. With right

sides together, pin the borders to the top and bottom edges of the quilt top, matching the center marks and ends and easing as necessary; stitch. Press the seams toward the border strips.

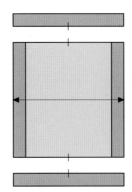

Measure center of quilt, side to side, including borders. Mark centers.

Borders with Mitered Corners

1. Estimate the finished outside dimensions of your quilt, including borders. For example, if your quilt top measures 35½" x 50½" across the center and you want a 5"-wide finished border, your quilt will measure 45" x 60" after the borders are attached. Cut border strips to these estimated dimensions plus at least ½" for seam allowances; adding 3" to 4" instead of ½" is safer because you will give yourself some leeway.

Note: If your quilt has multiple borders, sew the individual strips together and treat the resulting unit as a single border strip.

2. Fold the quilt in half and mark the center of the quilt edges. Fold each border strip in half and mark the center with a pin.

3. Measure the length and width of the quilt top through the horizontal and vertical centers. Note the measurements.

4. Place a pin at each end of the side border strips to mark the length of the quilt top. Repeat with the top and bottom borders.

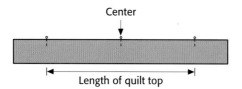

Center

Length of quilt top

5. Pin the borders to the quilt top, matching the centers. Line up the pins at each end of the border strip with the edges of the quilt. Stitch, beginning and ending the stitching ¼" from the raw edges of the quilt top. Repeat with the remaining borders.

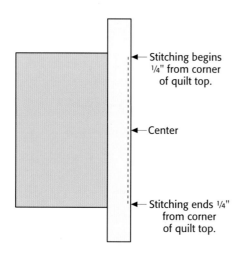

Stitching begins ¼" from corner of quilt top.

Center

Stitching ends ¼" from corner of quilt top.

6. Lay the first corner to be mitered on the ironing board. Fold under one border strip at a 45° angle to the other strip. Press and pin.

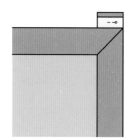

7. Fold the quilt with right sides together, lining up the edges of the border. If necessary, use a ruler to draw a pencil line on the crease to make it more visible. Stitch on the crease, sewing from the corner to the outside edge.

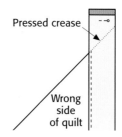

Pressed crease

Wrong side of quilt

8. Press the seam open and trim away excess border strips, leaving a ¼"-wide seam allowance.

9. Repeat with the remaining corners.

Layering and Basting

To layer and baste your quilt, place the backing on the table with the wrong side of the fabric facing up. If the table is large enough, you may want to tape the backing down with masking tape. Spread your batting over the backing, centering it, and smooth out any remaining folds.

Center the freshly pressed and marked quilt top on these two layers, right side up. Check all four sides to make sure there is adequate batting and backing. Stretch the backing to make sure it is still smooth.

The basting method you use depends on whether you will quilt by hand or by machine. Thread basting is generally used for hand quilting, while safety-pin basting is used for machine quilting.

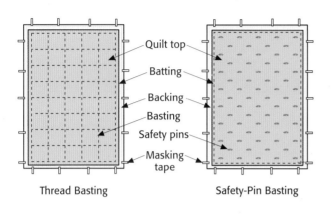

Thread Basting   Safety-Pin Basting

Binding

You can use bias strips or strips cut from the straight grain of fabric to make a French double-fold binding, which rolls over edges nicely and has two layers of fabric to resist wear.

To make straight-grain binding strips, cut 2½"-wide strips across the width of the fabric. You will need enough strips to go around the perimeter of the quilt, plus 10" for seams and the corners in a mitered fold.

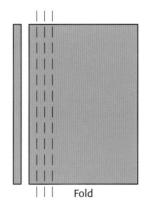

Fold

Some of the quilts in this book have a scrappy binding. For this binding, cut 2½"-wide strips in varying lengths from your quilt leftovers. These strips will need to be cut along the straight grain.

Seam the strips together until you have the length necessary for your quilt. Scrappy bindings look good on scrappy quilts and it's a good way to use up some of the leftovers.

For quilts with rounded corners, you will need to use bias-cut binding. To make bias-cut French binding, open up the binding fabric and lay it flat. Align the 45° line on your rotary cutting ruler with one of the selvage edges of the fabric. Cut along the ruler edge and trim off the corner. Cut the 2½"-wide strips, measuring from the edge of the initial bias cut.

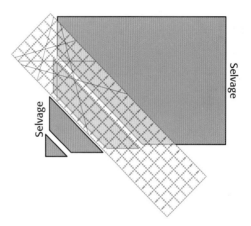

To join the strips and attach the binding, follow these steps:

1. With right sides together, join strips at right angles and stitch across the corner as shown. Trim excess fabric and press the seams open to make one long piece of binding.

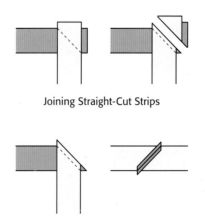

Joining Straight-Cut Strips

Joining Bias Strips

2. If necessary, trim one end of the strip at a 45° angle. Turn under ¼" and press. Fold the strip in half lengthwise, wrong sides together, and press.

3. Trim the batting and backing even with the quilt top.

4. Starting on one side of the quilt (not a corner) and using a ¼"-wide seam allowance, stitch the binding to the quilt, keeping the raw edges even with the quilt-top edge. End the stitching ¼" from the corner of the quilt and backstitch. Clip the thread.

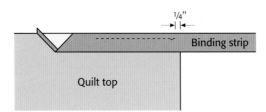

5. Turn the quilt so you will be stitching down the next side. Fold the binding up, away from the quilt, with raw edges aligned.

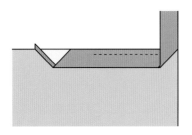

6. Fold the binding back down onto itself, even with the edge of the quilt top. Begin stitching at the corner, backstitching to secure the stitches.

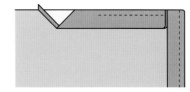

7. Repeat the process on the remaining edges and corners of the quilt. When you reach the beginning of the binding, stop stitching. Overlap the starting edge of the binding by about 1" and cut away any excess binding, trimming the end at a 45° angle. Tuck the end of the binding into the fold and finish the seam.

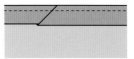

8. Fold the binding over the raw edges of the quilt to the back of the quilt, with the folded edge covering the row of machine stitching. Blindstitch the binding in place. A miter will form at each corner. Blindstitch the mitered corners in place.

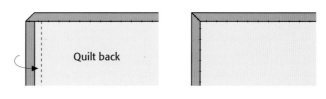

Plaid Obsession

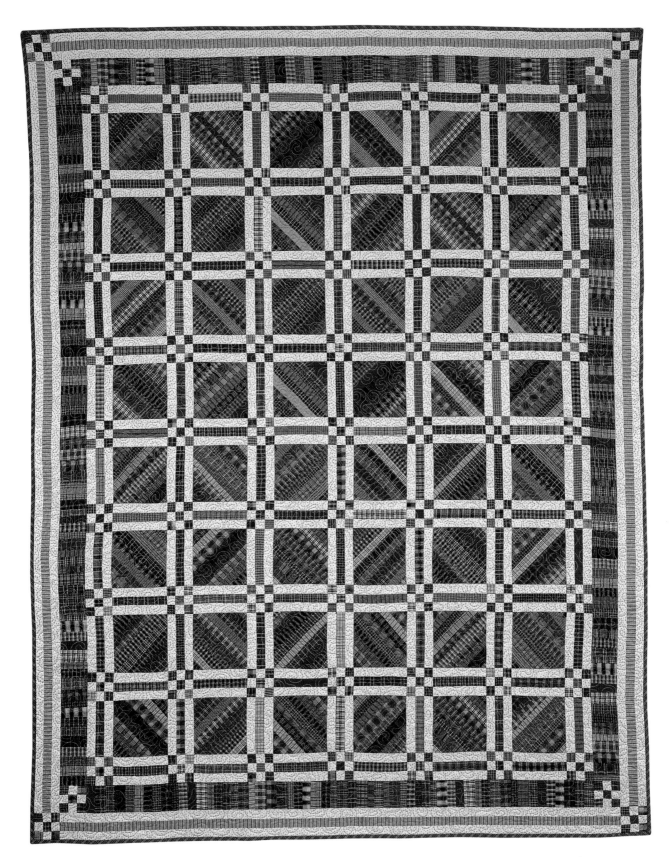

Finished quilt size: 69" x 87"~ Finished block sizes: Bias Square, 6" x 6"; Nine Patch, 3" x 3"

*I've made lots of cozy plaid quilts over the years,
so naturally, I have lots of plaid scraps. This quilt helped reduce
my collection of medium to dark plaid scraps, which blended together
beautifully. Use flannel for the backing, and I guarantee this quilt
will get used on cold winter evenings.*

Materials

Yardage is based on 42"-wide fabric.

5⅜ yds. *total* of assorted medium to dark plaid scraps *or* 22 fat quarters for string-pieced blocks, Nine Patch blocks, sashing, and inner border

3 yds. light-colored fabric for Nine Patch blocks, sashing, and outer border

½ yd. medium plaid for outer border

6 yds. fabric for backing

¾ yd. fabric for binding

77" x 95" piece of batting

Cutting

From the plaid scraps or fat quarters, cut a *total* of:
67 strips, 1½" x at least 21", for Nine Patch blocks and sashing

From the remaining plaid scraps or fat quarters, cut:
Approximately 164 strips that vary in width from 1" to 2½" and are at least 21" long. Strips that are less than 21" long but at least 12" long also will work, but you will need twice as many strips (refer to "String-Piecing Techniques" on page 11 for piecing and cutting instructions).

From the light-colored fabric, cut:
65 strips, 1½" x 42"; cut 49 of the strips in half widthwise to make 98 strips, 1½" x 21"

From the medium plaid for outer border, cut:
8 strips, 1½" x 42"

From the binding fabric, cut:
8 strips, 2½" x 42"

Making the String-Pieced Blocks

Refer to "String-Pieced Units for Bias Squares" on page 13.

1. Using approximately 120 of the plaid strips in varying widths, make 24 string-pieced units that measure at least 5" wide and 21" long, staggering the strips about 1". Make 12 units that stagger to the left and 12 units that stagger to the right. Press the seams in one direction. Trim each unit so that it measures exactly 5" wide.

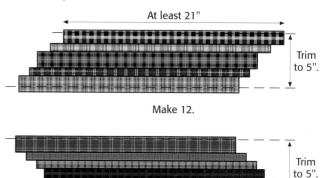

At least 21"

Trim to 5".

Make 12.

Trim to 5".

Make 12.

2. Place a right-staggered unit and a left-staggered unit right sides together. Stitch ¼" from both long edges.

3. Using a square ruler, line up the 6½" mark on both sides of the ruler with the bottom seam line as shown; cut along both sides of the ruler. Rotate the ruler and continue cutting, rotating the ruler in the opposite direction with every cut. Each set of paired strips will yield 4 blocks. Cut 48 blocks.

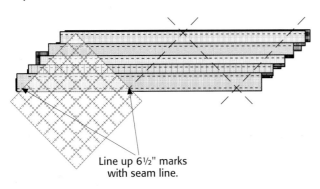

Line up 6½" marks
with seam line.

4. Remove any stitches at the point of each block. Open up each block and press the seam in one direction. The blocks should measure 6½" x 6½".

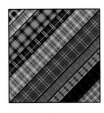

Make 48.

Making the Nine Patch Blocks and Sashing Units

1. Using the 1½" by at least 21" plaid strips and 1½" x 21" light strips, make strip sets A and B. To make strip set A, stitch a plaid strip to each side of 12 light strips as shown. Press the seams toward the plaid strips. Crosscut the strip sets into 142 segments, each 1½" wide.

To make strip set B, stitch a light strip to each side of 6 plaid strips. Press the seams toward the plaid strips. Crosscut the strip sets into 71 segments, each 1½" wide.

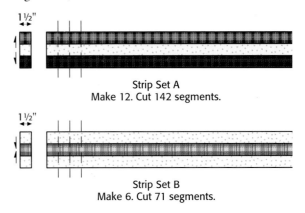

1½"

Strip Set A
Make 12. Cut 142 segments.

1½"

Strip Set B
Make 6. Cut 71 segments.

2. Stitch 2 strip set A segments and 1 strip set B segment together as shown to make a Nine Patch block. Make 71. Press the seams toward the strip set A segments. The blocks should measure 3½" x 3½".

Make 71.

3. Using the remainder of the 1½" x 21" strips, stitch a light strip to each side of a plaid strip to make strip set C. Make 37. Press the seams toward the plaid strips. Crosscut the strip sets into 110 segments, each 6½" wide, to make the sashing units.

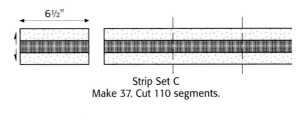

6½"

Strip Set C
Make 37. Cut 110 segments.

Tip

In order to make the most efficient use of your scraps, use your smaller pieces of plaid fabrics for the Nine Patch blocks and inner border.

Assembling the Quilt

Refer to "Assembly and Finishing" on pages 16–20.

1. Sew the string-pieced blocks, 63 of the Nine Patch blocks, and the sashing units into rows as shown, being sure to alternate the direction of the string-pieced blocks. Sew the rows together. Press the seams toward the sashing units.

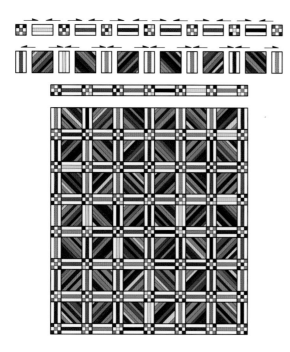

Tip

When sewing the blocks and sashing units together, always sew with the string-pieced blocks on the bottom. The pieces will ease together very nicely.

2. Measure the length and width of the quilt top through the center of the quilt and record the measurements. To make the inner pieced border, stitch several of the remaining plaid strips of varying widths together along the long edges to make a strip set. Make as many strip sets as necessary to use all of the strips. You can stitch as many or as few strips together as you'd like, but I've found that about 20 strips to a section makes a piece that is easy to work with. Press the seams in one direction. Crosscut the strip sets into 3½" segments.

3½"

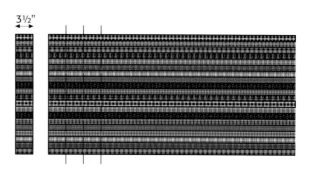

3. Stitch as many sections together as necessary to achieve the desired length for the side borders, trimming the strips to the correct length if necessary. Make 2. Repeat to make 2 pieced strips the length measured for the top and bottom borders. Stitch the pieced side borders to the quilt sides. Press the seams

toward the center of the quilt top. Stitch a Nine Patch block to each end of the pieced top and bottom border strips. Stitch the borders to the top and bottom edges of the quilt. Press the seams toward the center of the quilt top.

strip to each side of the plaid strips. Make 4 pieced border strips. Press the seams toward the plaid strips. Trim the strips to the correct lengths. Stitch the pieced side borders to the quilt sides. Press the seams toward the outer border. Stitch a Nine Patch block to each end of the pieced top and bottom border strips; stitch the strips to the top and bottom edges of the quilt top. Press the seams toward the outer border.

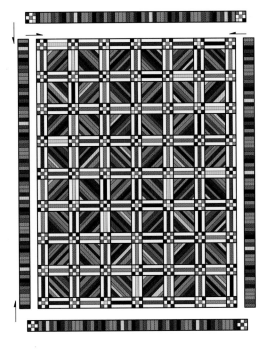

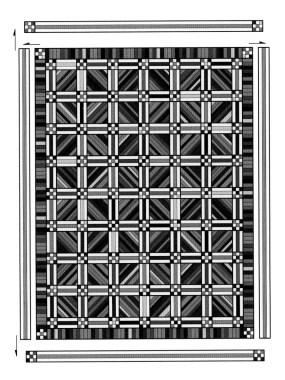

4. Measure the length and width of the quilt top through the centers again, including the borders you just added; record the measurements. To make the outer border pieces, stitch 2 medium plaid 1½" x 42" strips together end to end to make one long strip. Repeat to make 4 plaid strips. Stitch 2 light 1½" x 42" strips together end to end to make one long strip. Repeat to make 8 light strips. Stitch a light

5. Layer the quilt top with batting and backing; baste. Quilt as desired.

6. Bind the edges of the quilt.

Baby Fingers

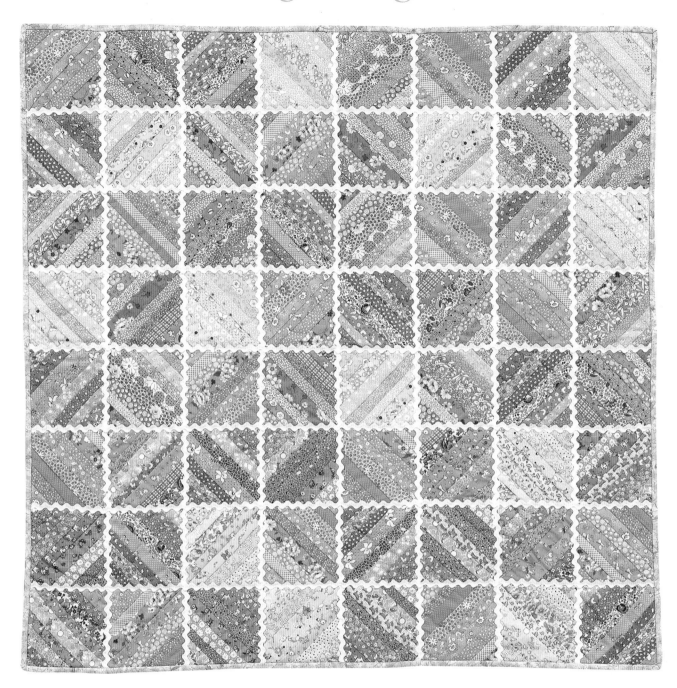

Finished quilt size: 44" x 44" ~ Finished block size: 5½" x 5½"

When I found out we were expecting another grandchild, I naturally wanted
to make a baby quilt. The '30s reproduction scraps and fat quarters I had seemed
to be a perfect choice. You will need ten prints each of five color families to make this quilt.
My quilt uses pink, blue, green, purple, and yellow prints.
If you don't have a lot of these fabrics on hand and the task of picking out
fifty prints seems too daunting, you can make every block multicolored
or just use two or three color families.

Materials

Yardage is based on 42"-wide fabric.

¾ yd. *total* of assorted scraps from each of 5 color families (pink, blue, green, purple, yellow) *or* ⅛ yd. *each* of 10 assorted prints from 5 color families for string-pieced blocks

3¼ yds. fabric for backing

½ yd. fabric for binding

52" x 52" piece of batting

7 packages (2½ yds. each) of jumbo-size white rickrack

Tip

If you choose to make every block multicolored, you will need a total of 3¾ yards of pastel scraps or 15 fat quarters. If you want to use just 3 color families, you will need ⅛ yard each of 10 prints from each color family.

Cutting

From the assorted scraps, cut:
Approximately 160 strips that vary in width from 1" to 2½" and are at least 20" long. Strips that are less than 20" long but at least 12" long also will work, but you will need twice as many strips (refer to "String-Piecing Techniques" on page 11 for piecing and cutting instructions).

From the binding fabric, cut:
5 strips, 2½" x 42"

Making the String-Pieced Blocks

Refer to "String-Pieced Units for Bias Squares" on page 13.

1. Using the assorted strips in varying widths, make 32 string-pieced units that measure at least 4¾" wide and 20" long, staggering the strips about 1". Make 16 units that stagger to the left and 16 units that stagger to the right. If you are using 5 color families, make 6 units for each of 4 color families (3 staggered to the left and 3 staggered to the right) and 8 units for 1 color family (4 staggered to the left and 4

staggered to the right). Press the seams in one direction. Trim each unit so that it measures exactly 4¾" wide.

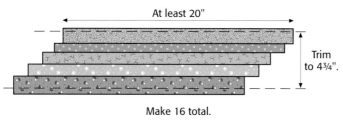

Make 16 total.

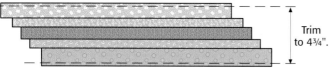

Make 16 total.

2. Place a right-staggered unit and a left-staggered unit right sides together. Stitch ¼" from both long edges.

3. Using a square ruler, line up the 6" mark on both sides of the ruler with the bottom seam line as shown; cut along both sides of the ruler. Rotate the ruler and continue cutting, rotating the ruler in the opposite direction with every cut. Each set of paired strips will yield 4 blocks. Cut a total of 64.

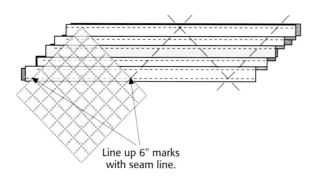

Line up 6" marks with seam line.

4. Remove any stitches at the point of each block. Open up each block and press the seam in one direction. The blocks should measure 6" x 6".

Assembling the Quilt

Refer to "Assembly and Finishing" on pages 16–20.

1. Sew the 64 string-pieced blocks into rows as shown, being sure to alternate the direction of the blocks. Press the seams in opposite directions from row to row. Sew the rows together. Press the seams in one direction.

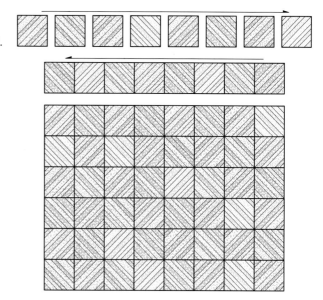

2. Stitch the rickrack over the horizontal seam lines first and then the vertical seam lines.

3. Layer the quilt top with batting and backing; baste. Quilt as desired.

4. Bind the edges of the quilt.

Tip

If you will be machine quilting your top, layer the quilt top with batting and backing, baste the layers together, and then apply the rickrack. These blocks are small, so that may be all the quilting you need.

Country Manor Charm

Finished quilt size: 57" x 73" ~ Finished block size: 8" x 8"

Dark, rich-looking scraps in country blues, purples, greens,
browns, and rusts have found their way into this pinwheel charmer.
In no time at all, you'll have this lap quilt ready for a long,
cozy evening. Save the corners you cut off the string-pieced blocks
and border to make "Starstruck" on page 34,
and most of the work for that quilt will already be done.

Materials

Yardage is based on 42"-wide fabric.

5 yds. *total* of assorted dark scraps or 20 fat quarters for string-pieced blocks

1¼ yds. light-colored fabric for border*

⅞ yd. of a different light-colored fabric for pinwheels

⅞ yd. *total* of assorted dark green scraps or 4 fat quarters for pinwheels

4¼ yds. fabric for backing

⅝ yd. fabric for straight-grain binding *or* 1 yd. for bias binding

65" x 81" piece of batting

Frosted template plastic or tracing paper

*Purchase an additional ⅝ yard if you plan to make "Starstruck."

Cutting

From the assorted dark scraps or fat quarters, cut:

Approximately 432 strips that vary in width from 1" to 2½" and are at least 9½" long. Strips that are at least 18" long will make 2 units, and you will need only half as many strips (refer to "String-Piecing Techniques" on page 11 for piecing and cutting instructions).

From the dark green scraps or fat quarters, cut:

5 strips, 5¼" x 42"; crosscut the strips into 32 squares, 5¼" x 5¼". Cut each square in half twice diagonally to yield 128 quarter-square triangles.

From the light-colored fabric for the pinwheels, cut:

5 strips, 5¼" x 42"; crosscut the strips into 32 squares, 5¼" x 5¼". Cut each square in half twice diagonally to yield 128 quarter-square triangles.

From the light-colored fabric for the border, cut:

2 strips, 16½" x 42". From the strips, cut:

14 strips, 5" x 16½"

4 squares, 5" x 5"

From the binding fabric, cut:

7 strips, 2½" x 42", for straight-grain binding or enough 2½"-wide bias strips to measure no less than 270" when pieced together. If you choose to make the quilt with rounded corners as shown on page 29, you must use bias binding.

Making the String-Pieced Blocks

Refer to "String-Piecing Techniques" on page 11.

1. Use the assorted dark scrap strips in varying widths to make 48 string-pieced units that measure at least 8½" wide and 9½" long. Press the seams in one direction. Trim each unit so that it measures exactly 8½" x 8½".

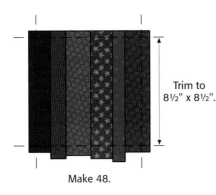

Trim to 8½" x 8½".

Make 48.

2. Sew 1 light triangle and 1 dark green triangle together along the short edges as shown, being sure that the green triangle is always on the right. Press the seam toward the green triangle. Make 128.

Make 128.

3. Trace the triangle template on page 33 onto a piece of template plastic or tracing paper and cut it out. Tape the template to the underside of a clear acrylic ruler, placing the long side of the triangle even with the ruler edge as shown. This will be referred to as the "corner cutter."

4. Trim 2 opposite corners of each string-pieced unit from step 1, using the corner cutter. To do this, place the string-pieced unit on your cutting mat so that the strips are horizontal, and place your ruler on the unit so that the corner cutter is even with the lower left corner. Cut along the edge of the ruler. Turn the unit and repeat with the opposite corner. Trim all 48 string-pieced units in this manner. Save the trimmed-off corners for making "Starstruck."

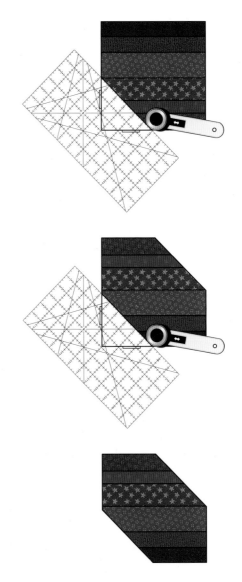

5. Stitch a triangle unit from step 2 to the trimmed corners of each string-pieced unit. Make 48 blocks. Press the seams toward the triangles.

Make 48.

Assembling the Quilt

Refer to "Assembly and Finishing" on pages 16–20.

1. Stitch the blocks into rows, orienting the blocks so the triangles are in alternate corners as shown. Press the seams in opposite directions from row to row. Sew the rows together. Press the seams in one direction.

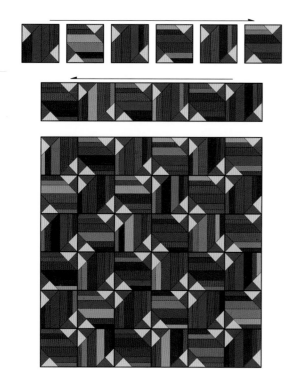

2. To make the pieced border, align the corner cutter with the corner of each light-colored 5" x 16½" strip as shown; cut off the corner. Repeat to cut off the corner at the opposite end of the strip as shown. Save the corners to use in "Starstruck."

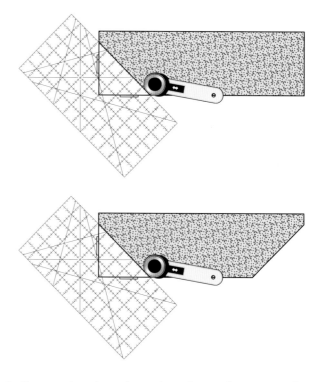

3. Sew a triangle unit to the trimmed corners of each strip as shown. Press the seams toward the triangles. Make 14.

Make 14.

4. Using the corner cutter, cut off 1 corner of each 5" square; stitch a triangle unit to each trimmed square as shown. Make 4.

Make 4.

5. Stitch 4 border pieces from step 3 together as shown for each of the side borders. Stitch the borders to the quilt sides. Stitch 3 border pieces from step 3 and 2 corner squares from step 4 together as shown for each of the top and bottom borders. Stitch the borders to the top and bottom edges of the quilt.

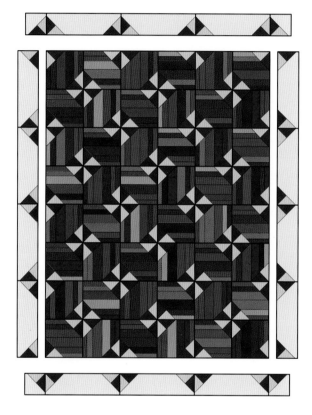

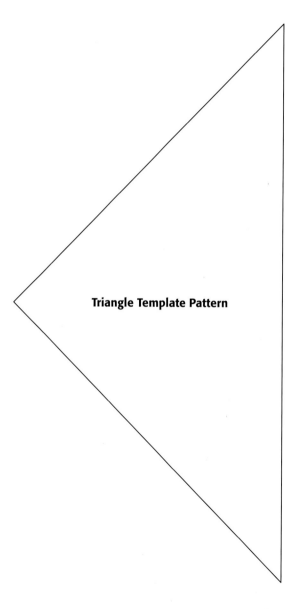

Triangle Template Pattern

6. Layer the quilt top with batting and backing; baste. Quilt as desired.

7. To make the quilt with rounded corners as shown on page 29, trim the corners, using a dinner plate as a guide.

8. Bind the edges of the quilt.

Starstruck

Finished quilt size: 24" x 36"~ Finished block size: 3" x 3"

*This wall hanging is made from the corners
that were cut off the string-pieced blocks and border pieces from
"Country Manor Charm" on page 29.*

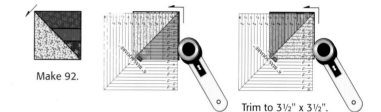

Materials

Yardage is based on 42"-wide fabric.

⅝ yd. border fabric used in "Country Manor Charm" for blocks and corner squares

92 string-pieced triangles left over from "Country Manor Charm" for blocks

28 border triangles left over from "Country Manor Charm" for blocks

1 yd. fabric for backing

⅜ yd. fabric for binding

28" x 40" piece of batting

Cutting

From the border fabric, cut:
4 strips, 4⅛" x 42". From the strips cut:

32 squares, 4⅛" x 4⅛"; cut each square in half once diagonally to yield 64 triangles. (These triangles, along with the 28 triangles left over from "Country Manor Charm," are enough for the 92 blocks.)

4 squares, 3½" x 3½"*

From the binding fabric, cut:
4 strips, 2½" x 42"

Read step 1 of "Directions" before cutting.

Directions

1. Sew a string-pieced triangle and a background triangle together along the long edges. Press the seam toward the background triangle. Make 92. Trim each square to 3½" x 3½".

Trimming is optional but it does ensure that all the blocks are the same size. If you choose not to trim your blocks, be sure to cut the 4 corner squares the same size as your blocks.

Make 92.

Trim to 3½" x 3½".

2. Sew the blocks and corner squares into rows as shown. Press the seams in opposite directions from row to row. Sew the rows together. Press the seams in one direction.

3. Referring to "Assembly and Finishing" on pages 16–20, layer the quilt top with batting and backing; baste. Quilt as desired. Bind the edges of the quilt.

Autumn Splendor

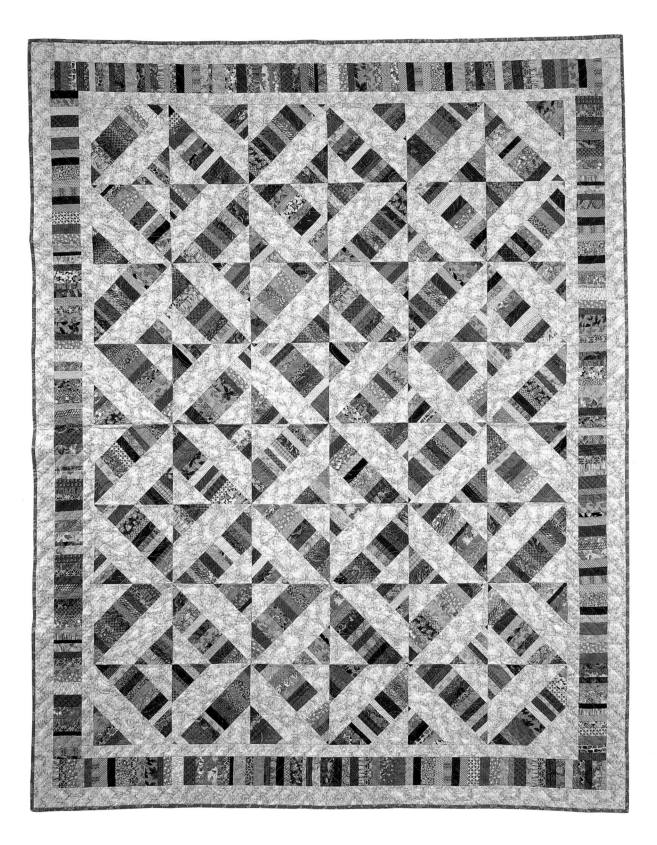

Finished quilt size: 75" x 95"~ Finished block size: 10" x 10"

You won't believe how easy this quilt is—it sure doesn't look it.
Just sew the strips together and cut out the block from the strips, and the
triangular shapes magically appear. You can use up lots of
smaller scraps while getting ready for winter with this cozy quilt.

Materials

Yardage is based on 42"-wide fabric.

7¼ yds. *total* of assorted autumn-colored scraps *or* 29 fat quarters for blocks and middle border

4¼ yds. light green for blocks, inner border, and outer border

6¼ yds. fabric for backing

¾ yd. fabric for binding

83" x 103" piece of batting

Cutting

From the assorted autumn-colored scraps or fat quarters, cut:
Approximately 1,266 strips that vary in width from 1" to 2½" and are at least 5" long. Strips that are at least 9" long will make 2 units, strips at least 13" long will make 3 units, and strips at least 17" long will make 4 units. You will need fewer strips if you use strips longer than 5" (refer to "String-Piecing Techniques" on page 11 for piecing and cutting instructions).

From the light green, cut:
24 strips, 4" x 42"

8 strips, 2" x 42"

9 strips, 3" x 42"

From the binding fabric, cut:
9 strips, 2½" x 42"

Making the String-Pieced Blocks

Refer to "String-Piecing Techniques" on page 11.

1. Using the autumn-colored strips, make 24 string-pieced units that measure at least 5" wide and 40" long. Press the seams in one direction. Trim each unit so that it measures exactly 4" wide.

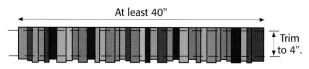

At least 40"

Trim to 4".

Make 24.

2. With right sides together, sew a 4"-wide light green strip to each string-pieced unit from step 1 as shown. Press the seam allowance toward the green strip.

3. Place 2 units from step 2 right sides together, alternating the position of the green strips as shown; stitch ¼" from both long edges. Repeat with the remaining step 2 units.

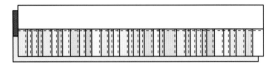

Place 2 units right sides together.

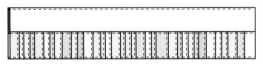

Stitch along both long edges.

4. Using a square ruler, line up the 10½" mark on both sides of the ruler with the bottom seam line as shown; cut along both sides of the ruler. Rotate the ruler and continue cutting, rotating the ruler in the opposite direction with every cut. Each set of paired strips will yield 4 blocks. Cut 48 blocks.

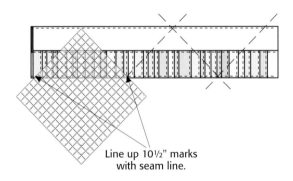

Line up 10½" marks with seam line.

5. Remove any stitches at the point of each block. Open up each block and press the seam toward the green strip. The blocks should measure 10½" x 10½".

Make 48.

Assembling the Quilt

Refer to "Assembly and Finishing" on pages 16–20.

1. Sew the blocks into rows as shown, being sure to alternate the direction of each block. Press the seams in opposite directions from row to row. Sew the rows together. Press the seams in one direction.

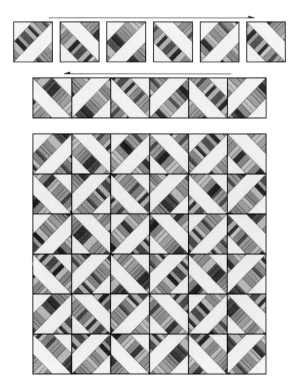

2. To make the inner border, refer to "Straight-Cut Borders" on page 17 to stitch the 2"-wide light green strips to the quilt edges.

3. Measure the length of the quilt top through the center of the quilt and record the measurement. To make the pieced middle border, stitch as many of the remaining autumn-colored strips together along the long edges as necessary to achieve a strip at least the length of the recorded measurement. Make 2. Trim the strips to 4" wide and the correct length. Stitch the strips to the sides of the quilt. Press the seams toward the inner border. In the same manner, measure the width of the quilt top through the center, including the borders you just added, and make 2 pieced strips for the top and bottom borders. Stitch the strips to the top and bottom edges of the quilt. Press the seams toward the inner border.

Tip

Use some of the strings from the waste sections in step 4 of "Making the String-Pieced Blocks" to make the middle border, as long as they are at least 4" long. This will take more time, but I had enough to make one border this way, and I felt good about using these strips.

4. For the outer border, repeat step 2 to stitch the 3"-wide light green strips to the quilt edges.

5. Layer the quilt top with batting backing; baste. Quilt as desired.

6. Bind the edges of the quilt.

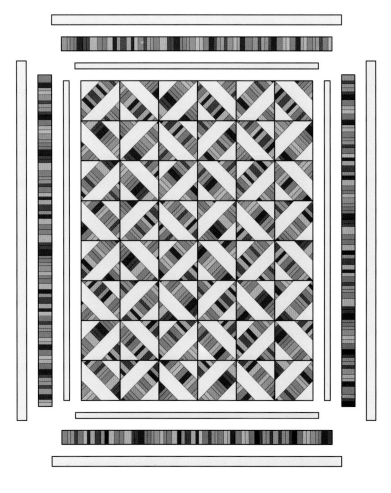

Finished quilt size: 79" x 96"~ Finished block size: 8½" x 8½"

I keep all of my Thimbleberries' fabric scraps together,
because all the colors blend so nicely from collection to collection.
This quilt is the result of an accumulation of many "fabrics past."
The green background fabric gives the quilt a warm, comfy feel and
produces an overall impression of green, even though many colors are present.

Materials

Yardage is based on 42"-wide fabric.

7⅜ yds. *total* of assorted medium to dark scraps *or* 30 fat quarters for blocks

4K yds. medium green for blocks and outer border

2 yds. dark green for blocks and inner border

7⅞ yds. fabric for backing

¾ yd. fabric for binding

87" x 104" piece of batting

Tip

You can change the primary color of this quilt easily by changing the color of the background fabric, so pick your favorite color for the background and use up lots of multicolored scraps.

Cutting

From the assorted medium to dark scraps or fat quarters, cut:
Approximately 640 strips that vary in width from 1" to 2½" and are at least 9" long. Strips that are at least 17" long will make 2 units, and you will need only half the amount of strips (refer to "String-Piecing Techniques" on page 11 for piecing and cutting instructions).

From the dark green, cut:
41 strips, 1½" x 42"

From the medium green, cut:
16 strips, 6" x 42"

9 strips, 5" x 42"

From the binding fabric, cut:
9 strips, 2½" x 42"

Making the String-Pieced Blocks

Refer to "String-Piecing Techniques" on page 11.

1. Using the assorted strips in varying widths, make 16 string-pieced units that measure at least 9" wide and 40" long. Press the seams in one direction. Trim each unit so that it measures exactly 8" wide.

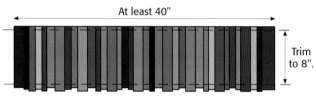

At least 40"

Trim to 8".

Make 16.

Tip

Use a medium gray thread when you're combining lots of different-colored fabrics in a quilt. The gray will blend well with all of the fabrics.

2. Sew a dark green 1½" x 42" strip to each side of a medium green 6" x 42" strip as shown. Make 16. Press the seams toward the dark green strips. The units should measure 8" x 42".

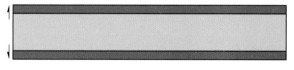

Make 16.

3. With right sides together, stitch each string-pieced unit from step 1 to a strip set from step 2; stitch ¼" from both long edges.

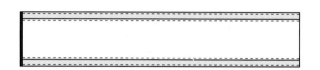

4. Using a square ruler, line up the 9" mark on both sides of the ruler with the bottom seam line as shown; cut along both sides of the ruler. Rotate the ruler and continue cutting, rotating the ruler in the opposite direction with every cut. Each set of paired strips will yield 5 blocks. Cut 80 blocks.

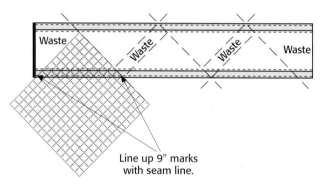

Waste Waste Waste Waste

Line up 9" marks with seam line.

5. Open up each block and press the seam toward the dark green strip. The blocks should measure 9" x 9".

Make 80.

Assembling the Quilt

Refer to "Assembly and Finishing" on pages 16–20.

1. Sew the blocks into rows as shown, being sure to alternate the direction of the blocks. Press the seams in opposite directions from row to row. Sew the rows together. Press the seams in the directions indicated.

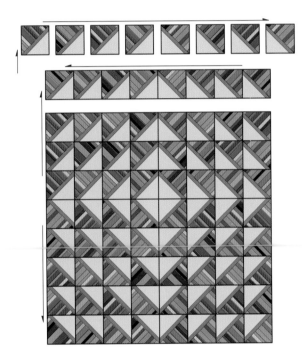

2. Referring to "Borders with Mitered Corners" on page 17, sew the remaining dark green 1½" x 42" strips and medium green 5" x 42" strips together along the long edges to make strips long enough for the borders. Stitch the borders to the quilt top.

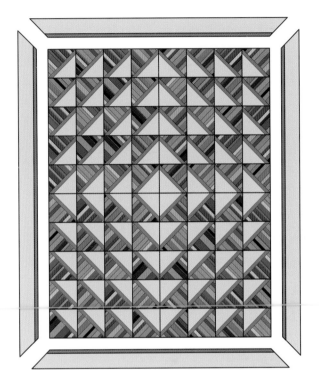

3. Layer the quilt top with batting and backing; baste. Quilt as desired.

4. Bind the edges of the quilt.

Angel Kisses

Finished quilt size: 50" x 60" ~ Finished block size: 10" x 10"

I was inspired to make this quilt one day while watching the snow fall.
I wanted to work with reds, and the snow motivated me to add the clean, crisp whites.
By the end of the day, the trees and ground outside
my sewing room were blanketed with several inches of snow, and
"Angel Kisses" was complete. Adding the white rickrack to cover
the seams really accents this pretty quilt.

Materials

Yardage is based on 42"-wide fabric.

5 yds. *total* of assorted red and pink scraps *or* 20 fat quarters for string-pieced blocks and appliqué blocks

¾ yd. white solid for appliqué blocks

3¾ yds. fabric for backing

⅝ yd. fabric for straight-grain binding *or* 1 yd. for bias binding

58" x 68" piece of batting

Paper-backed fusible transfer web

9 packages (2½ yds. each) of jumbo-size white rickrack

Cutting

From the assorted red and pink scraps or fat quarters, cut*:
Approximately 192 strips that vary in width from 1" to 2½" and are at least 20" long

From the white solid, cut:
2 strips, 11" x 42"; crosscut the strips to make 6 squares, 11" x 11"

From the binding fabric, cut:
6 strips, 2½" x 42", for straight-grain binding or enough 2½"-wide bias strips to measure no less than 230" when pieced together. If you choose to make the quilt with rounded corners as shown on page 44, you must use bias binding.

*Refer to step 1 of "Making the Heart Appliqué Blocks" on page 47 to cut the desired number of heart appliqués from the red and pink fabrics before cutting the strips.

Making the String-Pieced Blocks

Refer to "String-Pieced Units for Bias Squares" on page 13.

1. Using the red and pink strips in varying widths, make 24 string-pieced units that measure at least 8" wide and 20" long, staggering the strips about 1". Make 12 units that stagger to the left and 12 units that stagger to the right. Press the seams in one direction. Trim each unit so that it measures exactly 8" wide.

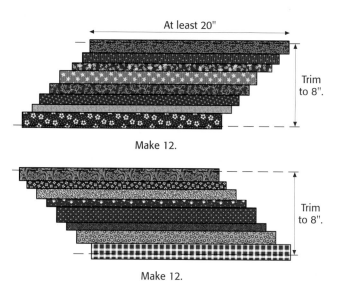

At least 20"

Trim to 8".

Make 12.

Trim to 8".

Make 12.

2. Place a right-staggered unit and a left-staggered unit right sides together. Stitch ¼" from both long edges.

3. Using a square ruler, line up the 10½" mark on both sides of the ruler with the bottom seam line as shown; cut along both sides of the ruler. Rotate the ruler and cut again. Each set of paired strips will yield 2 blocks. Cut 24 blocks.

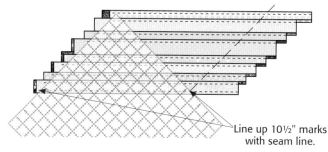

Line up 10½" marks with seam line.

4. Remove any stitches at the point of each block. Open each block and press the seam allowance in one direction. The blocks should measure 10½" x 10½".

Make 24.

Making the Heart Appliqué Blocks

1. Refer to "Fusible-Web Appliqué" on page 14 to prepare and cut the desired number and sizes of heart appliqués from the assorted red and pink scraps, using the patterns on page 48.

2. Arrange the appliqués as desired on the 6 white squares; fuse them in place. Buttonhole-stitch around each shape. Trim each square to 10½" x 10½".

Make 6.

Tip

The appliqué process tends to "draw up" the background fabric, and your finished piece may be smaller than desired. By cutting your background piece larger than required, you can trim it to the exact size needed after the appliqué is complete.

Assembling the Quilt

Refer to "Assembly and Finishing" on pages 16–20.

1. Sew the 24 string-pieced blocks and 6 appliqué blocks into rows as shown, being sure to alternate the direction of the string-pieced blocks. Press the seams in opposite directions from row to row. Stitch the rows together. Press the seams in one direction.

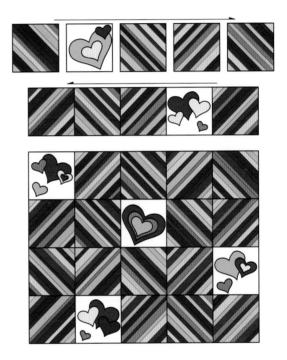

2. Stitch the rickrack over the horizontal seam lines first, and then the vertical seam lines. If you will be machine quilting your top, you can make this part of the machine quilting.

3. Layer the quilt top with batting and backing; baste. Quilt as desired.

4. To make the quilt with rounded corners as shown on page 44, trim the corners, using a dinner plate as a guide.

5. Bind the edges of the quilt.

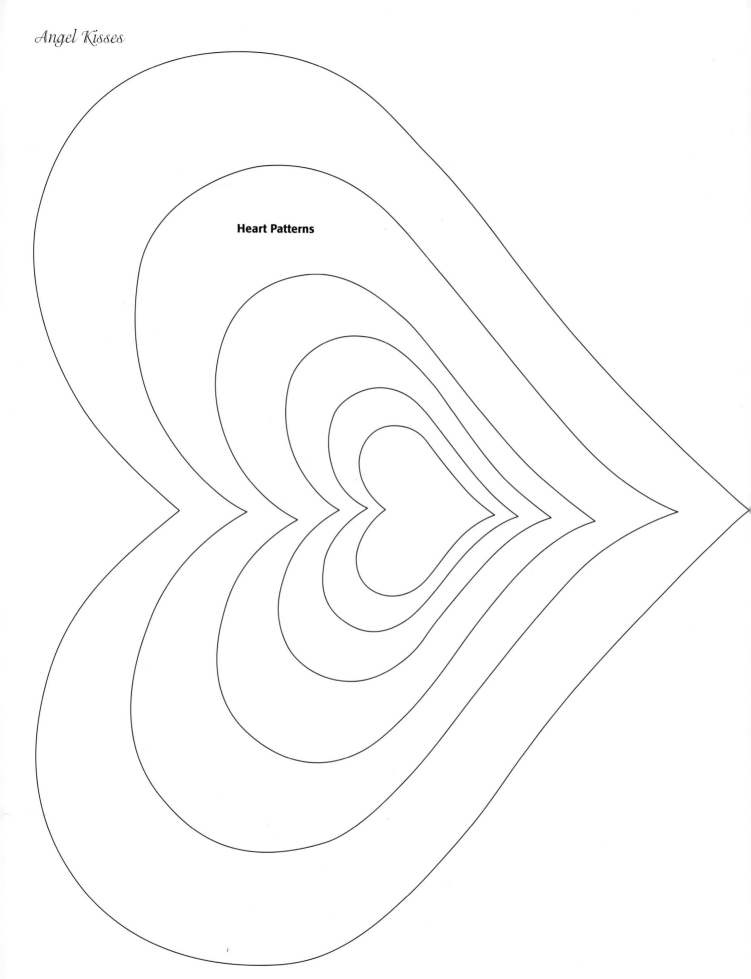

Heart Patterns

It's a Blue Sky Day

Finished quilt size: 46" x 63"~ Finished block size: 6" x 6"

Don't you love those days when there's not a cloud in the sky and the
sun is shining, and everything seems bright and cheery?
Those "blue sky days" inspired me to make a blue-and-yellow quilt.
My scraps had pale greens in them, too, so I pulled that color out in the
Nine Patch blocks. You'll love the easy technique for making
the string-pieced quarter-square triangle blocks.

Materials

Yardage is based on 42"-wide fabric.

3⅞ yds. blue for string-pieced blocks, inner border, and outer border

2⅛ yds. *total* of assorted blue and yellow scraps *or* 9 fat quarters for string-pieced blocks and middle border

⅝ yd. yellow for Nine Patch blocks and setting triangles

½ yd. light green for Nine Patch blocks and setting triangles

3½ yds. fabric for backing

⅝ yd. fabric for binding*

54" x 71" piece of batting

*Or, to make a scrappy binding like the one shown here, use fabric scraps (see step 6 of "Assembling the Quilt").

Cutting

From the assorted blue and yellow scraps or fat quarters, cut:
Approximately 56 strips that vary in width from 1" to 2½" and are at least 18" long. Strips that are less than 18" long but more than 11" long also will work, but you will need twice as many strips (refer to "String-Piecing Techniques" on page 11 for piecing and cutting instructions).

Approximately 28 strips that vary in width from 1" to 2½" and are at least 18½" long. If you have scraps that are at least 2½" long, they can also be used, but you will need enough strips that when pieced are equal to or longer than the border strip required (refer to step 3 of "Assembling the Quilt").

From the blue, cut:
4 strips, 5¼" x 42"; crosscut the strips into 25 squares, 5¼" x 5¼"

2 strips, 6½" x 42"; crosscut the strips into 8 squares, 6½" x 6½"

5 strips, 1½" x 42"

6 strips, 3½" x 42"

From the light green, cut:
5 strips, 2½" x 42"

From the yellow, cut:
3 strips, 2½" x 42"

2 strips, 4" x 42"; crosscut the strips into 14 squares, 4" x 4". Cut each square in half twice diagonally to yield 56 quarter-square triangles.

2 squares, 2" x 2"; cut each square in half once diagonally to yield 4 half-square triangles

From the binding fabric, cut:
6 strips, 2½" x 42"

Making the String-Pieced Blocks

Refer to "String-Pieced Units for Bias Squares" on page 13.

1. Using the approximately 56 blue and yellow strips in varying widths, make 14 string-pieced units that measure at least 4¼" wide and 18" long, staggering the strips about 1". Make 7 units that stagger to the left and 7 units that stagger to the right. Press the seams in one direction. Trim each unit so that it measures exactly 4¼" wide.

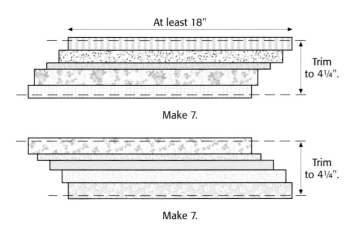

At least 18"

Trim to 4¼".

Make 7.

Trim to 4¼".

Make 7.

2. Place a right-staggered unit and a left-staggered unit right sides together. Stitch ¼" from both long edges.

3. Using a square ruler, line up the 5¼" mark on both sides of the ruler with the bottom seam line as shown; cut along both sides of the ruler. Rotate the ruler and continue cutting, rotating the ruler in the opposite direction with every other cut. Each pair of string-pieced units will yield 4 blocks. Cut 25 blocks.

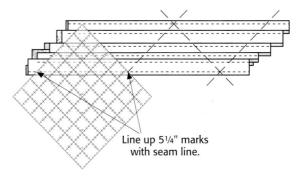

Line up 5¼" marks with seam line.

4. Remove any stitches at the point of each block. Open up each block and press the seam in one direction. The blocks should measure 5¼" x 5¼".

5. Alternately stitch 13 string-pieced blocks and 12 blue 5¼" squares together end to end, beginning and ending with a string-pieced block. Make another strip, using 13 blue squares and 12 string-pieced blocks, beginning and ending with a blue square. Press the seams toward the blue squares. Be sure to place the bias squares so the strips are going in the right direction.

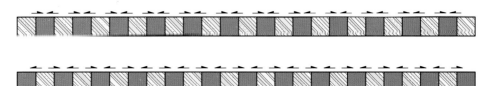

6. Place the strips from step 5 right sides together, pinning carefully to match the seams; stitch ¼" from both long edges.

7. Using a square ruler, line up the 45° line with the first vertical seam of the stitched strip from step 6. Line up the 6½" mark on both sides of the ruler with the bottom seam line; cut along both sides of the ruler. Rotate the ruler and continue cutting, rotating the ruler in the opposite direction with every cut. Cut 24 blocks.

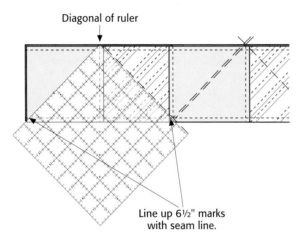

Diagonal of ruler

Line up 6½" marks with seam line.

8. Remove any stitches at the point of each block. Open up each block and press the seam in one direction. The blocks should measure 6½" x 6½".

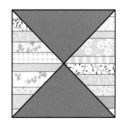

Make 24.

Making the Nine Patch Blocks

1. Using the 2½"-wide strips, stitch a light green strip to each side of a yellow strip to make strip set A. Press the seams toward the green strips. Crosscut the strip set into 14 segments, each 2½" wide.

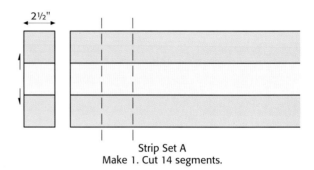

2½"

Strip Set A
Make 1. Cut 14 segments.

2. Cut 1 light green strip and 1 yellow strip in half widthwise. Stitch a yellow half strip to each side of the green half strip to make strip set B. Press the seams toward the green strip. Crosscut the strip set into 7 segments, each 2½" wide. Save the remaining green half strip for the Nine Patch setting triangles.

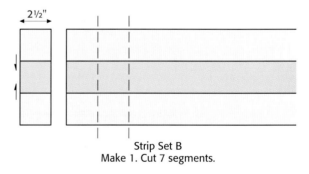

2½"

Strip Set B
Make 1. Cut 7 segments.

3. Stitch 2 strip set A segments and 1 strip set B segment together as shown. Press the seams toward the strip set A segments. Make 7 Nine Patch blocks. The blocks should measure 6½" x 6½".

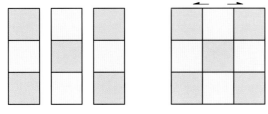

Make 7.

Making the Nine Patch Setting Triangles

1. Using the 2½" x 42" strips, stitch a light green strip and a yellow strip together along the long edges. Press the seam toward the green strip. Crosscut the strip set into 16 segments, each 2½" wide.

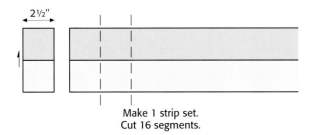

2½"

Make 1 strip set.
Cut 16 segments.

2. Cut the remaining light green 2½" x 42" strip and half strip into 20 squares, 2½" x 2½".

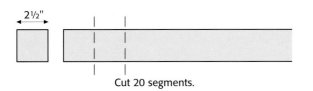

2½"

Cut 20 segments.

3. Sew a green square and a yellow quarter-square triangle together as shown. The triangles are larger than necessary so they will extend slightly beyond the seam line. Press the seams toward the green squares. Make 16 units.

Make 16.

4. Join 1 segment from step 1, 1 unit from step 3, and 2 yellow quarter-square triangles together as shown. Make 16 side setting triangles. Trim the triangles as shown if necessary.

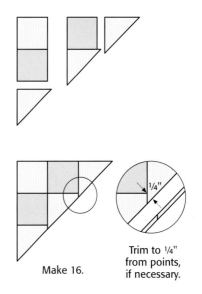

¼"

Make 16.

Trim to ¼"
from points,
if necessary.

5. To make the corner setting triangles, sew together one of the remaining green 2½" squares, 2 yellow quarter-square triangles, and 1 yellow half-square triangle as shown. Make 4.

Make 4.

Assembling the Quilt

Refer to "Assembly and Finishing" on pages 16–20.

1. Sew the string-pieced blocks, Nine Patch blocks, 6½" blue squares, and the corner and side setting triangles into diagonal rows as shown. Press the seams toward the blue squares, setting triangles, and Nine Patch blocks as shown. Stitch the rows together. Press the seams in one direction.

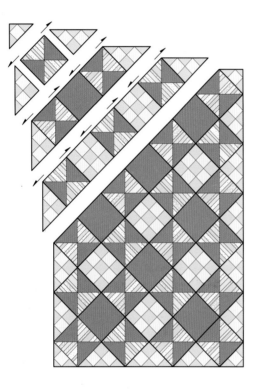

2. Refer to "Straight-Cut Borders" on page 17 to stitch the 1½"-wide blue strips to the quilt top for the inner border.

3. To make the middle border, measure the length of the quilt top through the center of the quilt and record the measurement. Stitch the 28 blue strips and yellow strips of varying widths together along the long edges to make a strip set. Press the seams in one direction. Crosscut the strip set into 2½"-wide sections. Stitch as many sections together as necessary to achieve the measurement recorded. Make 2.

Stitch the strips to the sides of the quilt top. Measure the width of the quilt top through the center, including the border strips you just added, and stitch together as many sections as needed to achieve the measurement. Make 2. Stitch the strips to the top and bottom edges of the quilt top.

4. Refer to "Straight-Cut Borders" on page 17 to stitch the 3½"-wide blue strips to the quilt top for the outer border.

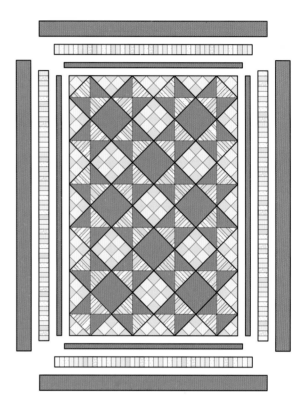

5. Layer the quilt top with batting and backing; baste. Quilt as desired.

6. Bind the edges of the quilt. If you wish to make a scrappy binding as shown, cut 2½"-wide strips of scraps in varying lengths. Sew these together to achieve the total length required to go around the quilt, and then bind the quilt as usual.

Winter Wishes

Finished quilt size: 74" x 74" ~ Finished block size: 12" x 12"

This sparkling star quilt is a great way to use up those smaller scraps
you've been saving from previous Christmas projects—or a great excuse to
go fabric shopping for some of the beautiful holiday fabrics available.
Although this quilt might look advanced, looks can be deceiving.
A beginning quilter could easily make this stunning quilt.

Materials

Yardage is based on 42"-wide fabric.

3⅜ yds. *total* of assorted Christmas scraps *or* 14 fat quarters for blocks and sashing

3⅛ yds. red for blocks and border

1¾ yds. yellow for sashing and border

5 yds. fabric for backing

¾ yd. fabric for straight-grain binding *or* 1 yd. for bias binding

82" x 82" piece of batting

Frosted template plastic or tracing paper

12½" x 12½" clear acrylic ruler

Cutting

From the assorted Christmas scraps or fat quarters, cut:

Approximately 288 strips that vary in width from 1" to 2½" and are at least 4¼" long. These strips will be used to make the units for the string-pieced blocks. Strips that are at least 7½" long will make 2 units, strips at least 10¾" long will make 3 units, and strips at least 14" long will make 4 units. You will need fewer strips if you use strips longer than 4¼" (refer to "String-Piecing Techniques" on page 11 for piecing and cutting instructions).

Approximately 520 strips that vary in width from 1" to 2½" and are at least 5½" long. These strips will be used to make the sashing units. Strips that are at least 10" long will make 2 units, strips at least 14½" long will make 3 units, and strips at least 19" long will make 4 units. You will need fewer strips if you use strips longer than 5½" (refer to "String-Piecing Techniques" on page 11 for piecing and cutting instructions).

From the red, cut:

6 strips, 11½" x 42"; crosscut the strips into 16 squares, 11½" x 11½". Cut each square in half once diagonally to yield 32 triangles.

9 strips, 3½" x 42"; crosscut the strips into:

      16 strips, 3½" x 12½"

      20 rectangles, 3½" x 4½"

      4 squares, 3½" x 3½"

From the yellow, cut:

4 strips, 4½" x 42"; crosscut the strips into 25 squares, 4½" x 4½"

14 strips, 2½" x 42"; crosscut the strips into 200 squares, 2½" x 2½"

From the binding fabric, cut:

8 strips, 2½" x 42", for straight-grain binding or enough 2½"-wide bias strips to measure no less than 305" when pieced together. If you choose to make the quilt with rounded corners as shown on page 55, you must use bias binding.

Making the String-Pieced Blocks

1. Referring to "String-Piecing Techniques" on page 11, use the approximately 288 strips that vary in width and are at least 4¼" long to make 16 string-pieced units that measure at least 4¼" wide and 18" long. Press the seams in one direction. Trim each unit so that it measures exactly 3¼" wide.

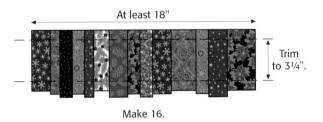

At least 18"

Trim to 3¼".

Make 16.

2. Fold each string-pieced unit in half widthwise, wrong sides together; finger-press the folded edge at each end to make a crease. Fold each red triangle in half, right sides together; finger-press the fold along the long edge to make a crease. Stitch a red triangle to the long edges of each string-pieced unit as shown, matching the crease marks. Stitch with the triangle on top. Press the seams toward the triangles.

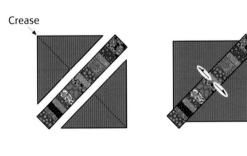

Crease

Tip

By folding one piece right sides together and the other piece wrong sides together, the top crease will sink into the bottom crease when you place the two pieces together, and they will stay together much easier.

3. Trace the template on page 59 onto a piece of template plastic or tracing paper and cut it out. Tape the template to the underside of the 12½"-square clear acrylic ruler as shown.

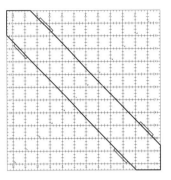

4. Place the ruler over a unit from step 2, lining up the template with the string-pieced section. Trim 2 adjacent sides even with the ruler; rotate the unit 180°, re-align the ruler, and trim the remaining 2 sides. The block should measure 12½" x 12½". Repeat with the remaining 15 string-pieced units.

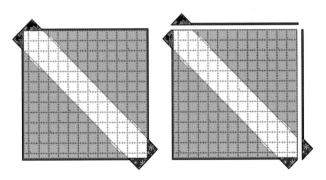

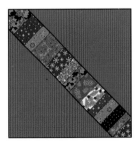

Make 16.

Making the Sashing Units

1. Referring to "String-Piecing Techniques" on page 11, use the approximately 520 strips that vary in width and are at least 5½" long to make 40 string-pieced units that measure at least 5½" wide and 12½" long. Press the seams in one direction. Trim each unit so that it measures exactly 4½" x 12½".

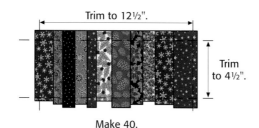

Trim to 12½".
Trim to 4½".

Make 40.

2. Draw a diagonal line on the wrong side of each 2½" yellow square as shown. Most of the squares will be used in the sashing, and the remaining ones will be used in the border.

3. Place a yellow square from step 2 on one corner of a string-pieced unit from step 1, right sides together; sew on the drawn line. Trim ¼" from the seam, then press the triangle toward the corner. Repeat with the remaining 3 corners. Make 40 sashing units.

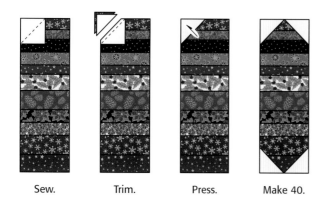

Sew.   Trim.   Press.   Make 40.

Assembling the Quilt

Refer to "Assembly and Finishing" on pages 16–20.

1. Join the 16 blocks, 40 sashing units, and 25 yellow 4½" squares into rows as shown. Press the seams toward the blocks and yellow squares. Sew the rows together. Press the seams toward the blocks.

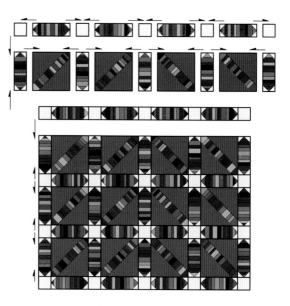

2. For the border, place one of the remaining 2½" yellow squares on one corner of a red 3½" x 4½" rectangle, right sides together, and sew on the drawn line. Trim ¼" from the seam line. Press the triangle toward the corner. Repeat for the opposite corner on the same long edge of the rectangle. Make 20 units.

Make 20.

3. To make the borders, stitch 5 units from step 2 and 4 red 3½" x 12½" strips together as shown. Press the seams toward the red strips. Make 4. Stitch a strip to each side of the quilt top. Sew a 3½" red square to each end of the remaining 2 strips. Stitch the strips to the top and bottom edges of the quilt top.

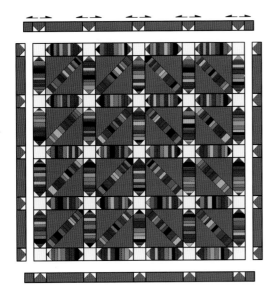

4. Layer the quilt top with batting and backing; baste. Quilt as desired.

5. To make the quilt with rounded corners as shown on page 55, trim the corners, using a dinner plate as a guide.

6. Bind the edges of the quilt.

Cutting Template Pattern

Place on fold.

Bunny Love

Finished quilt size: 54" x 54" ~ Finished block sizes: String-Pieced, 5½" x 5½";
Bunny Appliqué, 11" x 11"

*I made this quilt for my niece Heather Willoughby,
who designed the cute, floppy-eared bunnies. This makes a great
Easter wall hanging or a baby quilt. Change the color scheme to blues
and yellows for an adorable quilt for a baby boy.*

Materials

Yardage is based on 42"-wide fabric.

2⅞ yds. *total* of assorted pink, green, and yellow scraps *or* 12 fat quarters for string-pieced blocks

2½ yds. light-colored fabric for string-pieced blocks, appliqué blocks, and outer border

⅜ yd. pink for inner border

4 yds. fabric for backing

⅝ yd. fabric for straight-grain binding *or* ⅞ yd. for bias binding

62" x 62" piece of batting

Frosted template plastic or tracing paper

6" x 6" clear acrylic ruler

Paper-backed fusible transfer web

Water-soluble marker or pencil

Gray-green embroidery floss

Embroidery needle

Cutting

From the assorted pink, green, and yellow scraps, cut*:
Approximately 396 strips that vary in width from 1" to 2½" and are at least 5" long. Strips that are at least 9" long will make 2 units, strips at least 13" long will make 3 units, and strips at least 17" long will make 4 units. You will need fewer strips if you use strips longer than 5" (refer to "String-Piecing Techniques" on page 11 for piecing and cutting instructions).

From the light-colored fabric, cut:
6 strips, 4½" x 42"; crosscut the strips into 44 squares, 4½" x 4½". Cut each square in half once diagonally to yield 88 half-square triangles.

2 strips, 12" x 42"; crosscut the strips into 5 squares, 12" x 12"

6 strips, 4½" x 42"

From the pink fabric, cut:
6 strips, 1½" x 42"

From the binding fabric, cut:
6 strips, 2½" x 42", for straight-grain binding or enough 2½"-wide bias strips to measure no less than 226" when pieced together. If you choose to make the quilt with rounded corners as shown on page 60, you must use bias binding.

*Refer to step 1 of "Making the Appliqué Blocks" on page 63 to cut the required appliqué pieces from the pink, green, and yellow scraps or fat quarters before cutting the strips.

Making the String-Pieced Blocks

Refer to "String-Piecing Techniques" on page 11.

1. Use the pink, green, and yellow strips to make 44 string-pieced units that measure at least 5" wide and 8½" long. Press the seams in one direction. Trim each unit so that it measures exactly 4" wide.

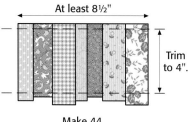

Make 44.

2. Fold each string-pieced unit in half widthwise, wrong sides together; finger-press the folded edge to make a crease. Fold each light-colored triangle in half along the longest edge, right sides together; finger-press the fold at the long edge to make a crease. Stitch a triangle to the long edges of each string-pieced unit as shown, matching the crease marks. Stitch with the triangle on top. Press the seams toward the triangles.

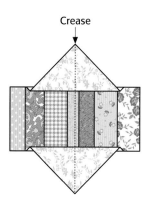

Crease

Tip

If you are good at eyeballing these pieces so that they are centered, you can avoid the finger creases. The pieces are oversized and will be trimmed down to exact size, so there is room for some error. See which method works best for you.

3. Trace the template on page 64 onto a piece of template plastic or tracing paper and cut it out. Tape the template to the underside of a 6"-square clear acrylic ruler as shown.

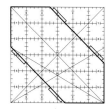

4. Place the ruler over a unit from step 2, lining up the template with the string-pieced section. Trim 2 adjacent sides even with the ruler; rotate the unit 180°, realign the ruler, and trim the remaining 2 sides. The block should measure 6" x 6". Repeat with the remaining 43 blocks.

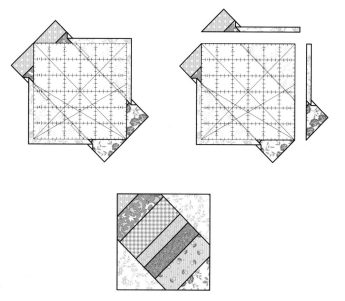

Make 44.

Making the Appliqué Blocks

1. Refer to "Fusible-Web Appliqué" on page 14 to prepare and cut the bunny appliqués from the assorted pink, green, and yellow scraps, using the patterns on pages 65 and 66. Cut 5 each of the bunny head, right ear, and left ear; cut 3 each of the remaining sitting bunny pieces; and 2 each of the remaining standing bunny pieces. Using a water-soluble marker or pencil, transfer the face design to each bunny head.

2. Refer to the appliqué placement diagrams on page 66 to arrange the pieces on the light-colored 12" squares so that the completed bunny is centered. Make 3 sitting bunnies and 2 standing bunnies. Fuse the pieces in place. Buttonhole stitch around each piece. Trim each square to 11½" x 11½".

3. Using 2 strands of gray-green floss, work a stem stitch around the eyes, nose, and mouth. Fill in the pupils and nose with satin stitching.

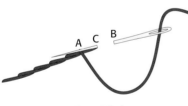

Stem Stitch

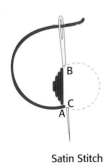

Satin Stitch

Assembling the Quilt

Refer to "Assembly and Finishing" on pages 16–20.

1. Sew the 44 string-pieced blocks and 5 appliqué blocks into rows as shown. Alternate the direction of the string-pieced blocks. Press the seams in the directions indicated. Sew the rows together. Press the seams in one direction.

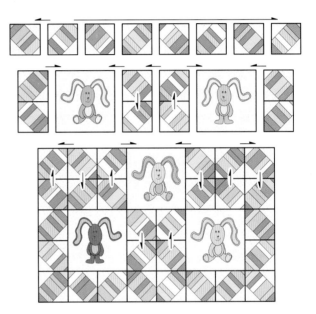

2. Referring to "Borders with Mitered Corners" on page 17, stitch the 1½" x 42" pink strips and light-colored 4½" x 42" strips together along the long edges to make strips long enough for the borders. Stitch the borders to the quilt top.

3. Layer the quilt top with batting and backing; baste. Quilt as desired.

4. To make the quilt with rounded corners as shown on page 60, trim the corners, using a dinner plate as a guide.

5. Bind the edges of the quilt.

Cutting Template Pattern

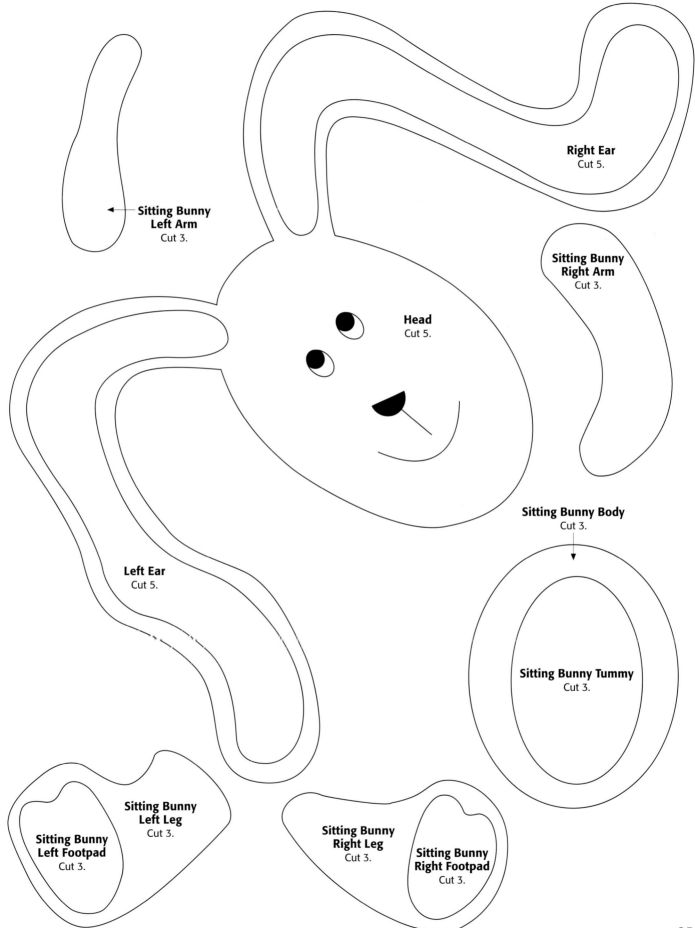

Right Ear
Cut 5.

Sitting Bunny
Left Arm
Cut 3.

Sitting Bunny
Right Arm
Cut 3.

Head
Cut 5.

Sitting Bunny Body
Cut 3.

Left Ear
Cut 5.

Sitting Bunny Tummy
Cut 3.

Sitting Bunny
Left Leg
Cut 3.

Sitting Bunny
Left Footpad
Cut 3.

Sitting Bunny
Right Leg
Cut 3.

Sitting Bunny
Right Footpad
Cut 3.

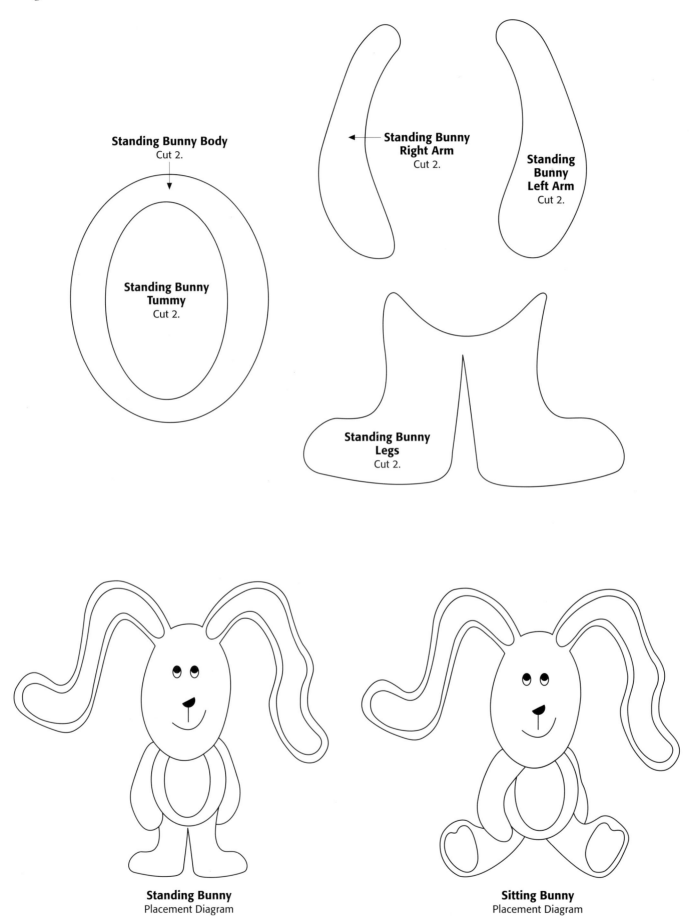

Standing Bunny Body
Cut 2.

Standing Bunny Tummy
Cut 2.

Standing Bunny Right Arm
Cut 2.

Standing Bunny Left Arm
Cut 2.

Standing Bunny Legs
Cut 2.

Standing Bunny
Placement Diagram

Sitting Bunny
Placement Diagram

On the Wild Side

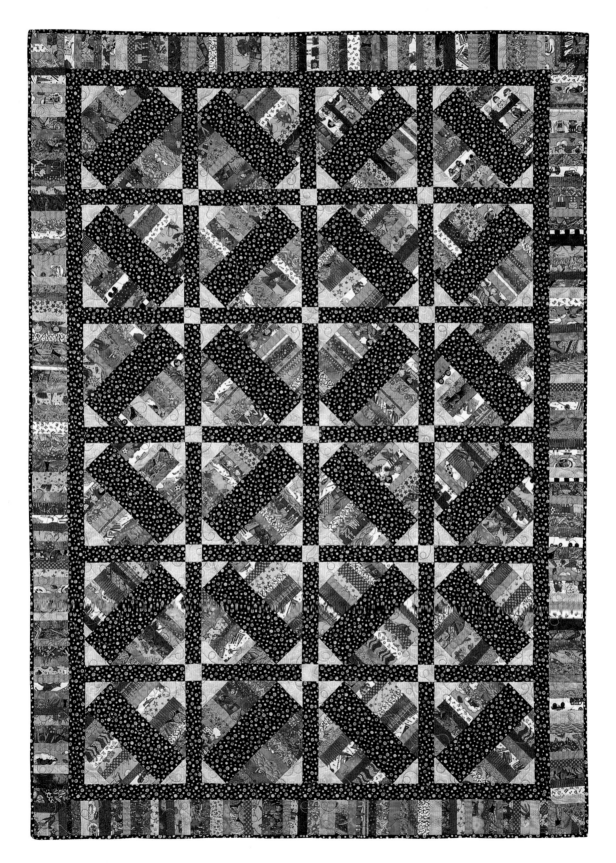

Finished quilt size: 66½" x 94½" ~ Finished block size: 12" x 12"

My grandchildren loved going through all the scraps from the quilts

I had made for them and reminiscing about each piece.

Even the youngest ones could pick out pieces from their special quilts.

Now, the problem is, who gets this quilt, since they all want it?

Maybe I'll just keep it for all of them to use when they visit me.

Materials

Yardage is based on 42"-wide fabric.

6¾ yds. *total* of assorted bright-colored scraps *or* 27 fat quarters for blocks and outer border

3 yds. black print for blocks, sashing, and inner border

1⅛ yds. yellow print for blocks and sashing corner squares

6¼ yds. fabric for backing

¾ yd. fabric for binding

74" x 102" piece of batting

Frosted template plastic or tracing paper

12½" x 12½" clear acrylic ruler

Cutting

From the assorted bright-colored scraps or fat quarters, cut:
Approximately 997 strips that vary in width from 1" to 2½" and are at least 5¾" long. Strips that are at least 10½" long will make 2 units, strips at least 15¼" long will make 3 units, and strips at least 20" long will make 4 units. You will need fewer strips if you use strips longer than 5¾" (refer to "String-Piecing Techniques" on page 11 for piecing and cutting instructions).

From the black print, cut:
8 strips, 4¾" x 42"; crosscut the strips into 24 strips, 4¾" x 13¼"

22 strips, 2½" x 42"; crosscut 13 of the strips into 38 pieces, 2½" x 12½". Set the rest of the strips aside for the inner border.

From the yellow print, cut:
6 strips, 5" x 42"; crosscut the strips into 48 squares, 5" x 5". Cut each square in half once diagonally to yield 96 triangles.

1 strip, 2½" x 42"; crosscut the strip into 15 squares, 2½" x 2½"

From the binding fabric, cut:
9 strips, 2½" x 42"

Making the String-Pieced Blocks

1. Referring to "String-Piecing Techniques" on page 11, use the assorted bright-colored strips to make 48 string-pieced units that measure at least 5¾" wide and 14½" long. Press the seams in one direction. Trim each unit so that it measures exactly 4¾" wide. Set the remaining bright-colored strips aside for the outer border.

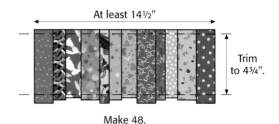

At least 14½"

Trim to 4¾".

Make 48.

2. Fold each black 4¾" x 13¼" strip in half lengthwise, wrong sides together; finger-press each end along the fold to make a crease. Fold each yellow triangle in half along the long edge, right sides together; finger-press the fold at the long edge to make a crease. Stitch a triangle to each end of the black strip as shown, matching the crease marks and stitching with the triangle on top. Set the remaining triangles aside to use in step 4. Press the seams toward the triangles. Trim the triangle sides even with the black strip. Make 24 units.

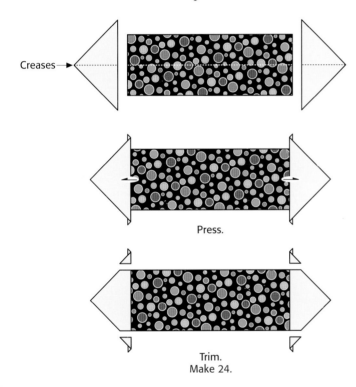

Press.

Trim.
Make 24.

3. Fold each string-pieced unit in half widthwise, right sides together; finger-press the folded edge to make a crease. Fold each unit from step 2 in half widthwise, wrong sides together; finger-press the folded edge to make a crease. Stitch a string-pieced unit to each side of each step 2 unit as shown, matching the crease

marks. Press the seams toward the black strip. Make 24 units.

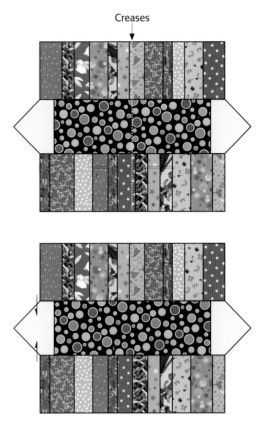

Creases

4. Sew 2 of the remaining creased yellow triangles from step 2 to the sides of each unit from step 3 as shown, matching the crease marks. Press the seams toward the triangles. Make 24.

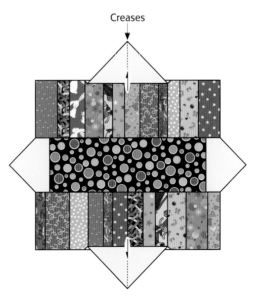

Creases

Tip

If you are good at eyeballing these pieces so that they are centered, you can avoid all the finger creasing. The pieces are oversized and will be trimmed down to exact size, so there is room for some error. See which method works best for you.

5. Trace the template on page 72 onto a piece of template plastic or tracing paper and cut it out. Tape the template to the underside of a 12½" square ruler as shown.

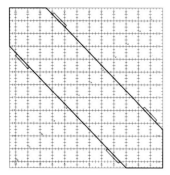

6. Place the ruler over a unit from step 4, lining up the template with the black strip and yellow triangles as shown. Trim 2 adjacent sides even with the ruler; rotate the unit 180°, realign the ruler, and trim the remaining 2 sides. The block should measure 12½" x 12½". Repeat with the remaining 23 blocks.

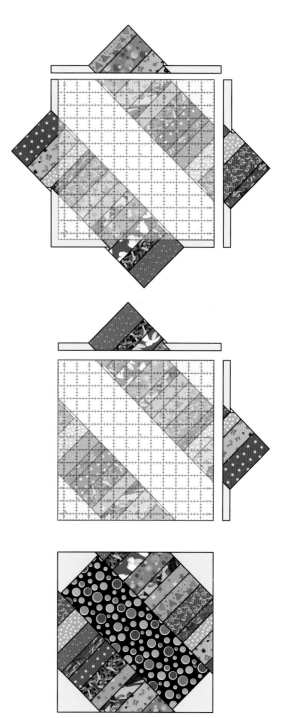

Make 24.

Assembling the Quilt

Refer to "Assembly and Finishing" on pages 16–20.

1. Sew the 24 string-pieced blocks, the 38 black 2½" x 12½" sashing strips, and the 15 yellow 2½" squares into rows as shown, being sure to alternate the direction of the string-pieced blocks. Press the seams toward the sashing strips. Sew the rows together. Press the seams toward the sashing rows.

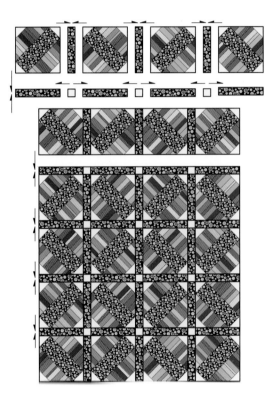

2. Stitch the remaining bright-colored strips together along the long edges to make strips 3" to 4" longer than needed for the outer border. Trim each border strip to 4¾" wide. Piece the black 2½"-wide inner border strips together as needed to make strips in lengths that correspond to each outer border strip. Stitch the outer and inner border strips together along the long edges to make the border unit. Referring to "Borders with Mitered Corners" on page 17, stitch the border unit to the quilt top.

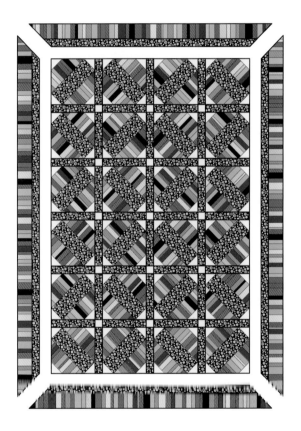

3. Layer the quilt top with batting and backing; baste. Quilt as desired.

4. Bind the edges of the quilt.

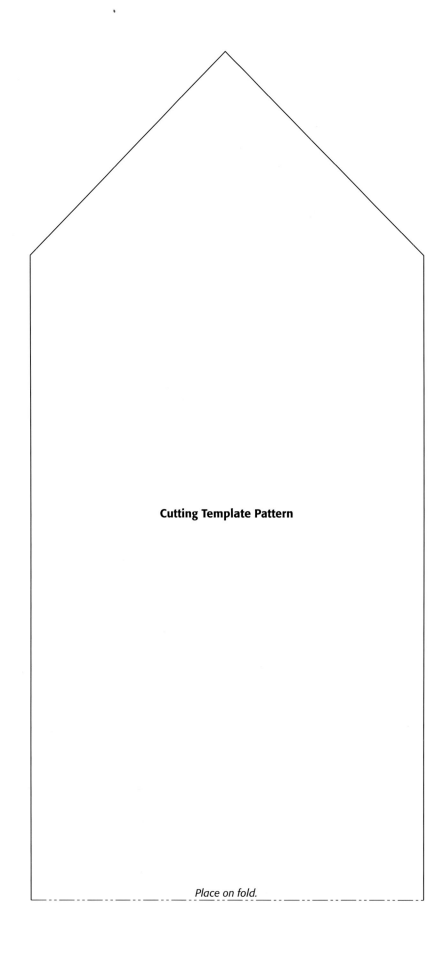

Cutting Template Pattern

Place on fold.

The Elegance of Red

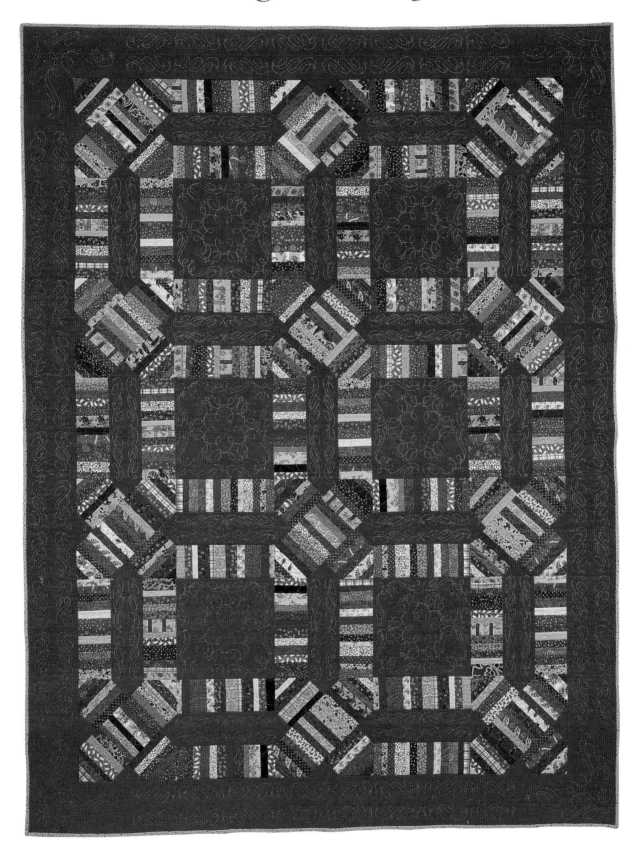

Finished quilt size: 72" x 96" ~ Finished block size: 12" x 12"

The red background fabric makes this quilt feel rich, vibrant, and alive.
All kinds of scraps can go into the string-pieced blocks,
but the quilt will still appear to be red. Change the color of the
background for a completely different quilt. You will be surprised
at how quickly the "X" and Rail Fence blocks go together.

Materials

Yardage is based on 42"-wide fabric.

6¼ yds. *total* of assorted multicolored scraps *or* 25 fat quarters for blocks

3¾ yds. red for blocks and border

6½ yds. fabric for backing

¾ yd. fabric for binding

80" x 104" piece of batting

Frosted template plastic or tracing paper

12½" x 12½" clear acrylic ruler

Cutting

From the assorted multicolored scraps or fat quarters, cut:

Approximately 372 strips that vary in width from 1" to 2½" and are at least 7" long. These strips are used to make the "X" blocks. Strips that are at least 13" long will make 2 units, and strips at least 19¼" long will make 3 units. You will need fewer strips if you use strips longer than 7" (refer to "String-Piecing Techniques" on page 11 for piecing and cutting instructions).

Approximately 425 strips that vary in width from 1" to 2½" and are at least 5½" long. These strips are used to make the Rail Fence blocks. Strips that are at least 10" long will make 2 units, strips at least 14½" long will make 3 units, and strips at least 19" long will make 4 units. You will need fewer strips if you use strips longer than 5½" (refer to "String-Piecing Techniques" on page 11 for piecing and cutting instructions).

From the red, cut:

2 strips, 6" x 42"; crosscut the strips into 12 squares, 6" x 6". Cut each square in half twice diagonally to yield 48 triangles.

6 strips, 4½" x 42"; crosscut the strips into 17 pieces, 4½" x 12½"

2 strips, 12½" x 42"; crosscut the strips into 6 squares, 12½" x 12½"

9 strips, 6½" x 42"

From the binding fabric, cut:

9 strips, 2½" x 42"

Tip

To avoid piecing the strips for the border, cut them from the lengthwise grain of the fabric before cutting any other pieces. Just cut 4 strips, each 6½" by the length of the fabric. The lengthwise grain is also more stable than the crosswise grain, and cutting the strips in this manner can eliminate wavy borders.

Making the String-Pieced "X" Blocks

1. Referring to "String-Piecing Techniques" on page 11, use the multicolored strips that are at least 7" long to make 12 string-pieced units that measure at least 7" wide and 18" long and 24 units that measure at least 7" wide and 6½" long. Press the seams in one direction. Trim each unit so that it measures exactly 6⅛" wide.

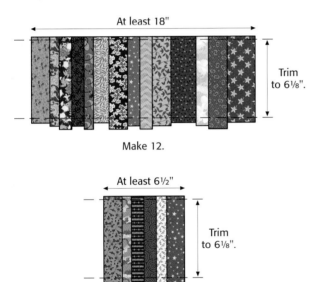

At least 18"

Trim to 6⅛".

Make 12.

At least 6½"

Trim to 6⅛".

Make 24.

2. Stitch a red triangle to opposite sides of each of the shorter units from step 1 as shown. Make 24. Press the seams toward the triangles.

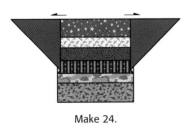

Make 24.

3. Fold each long string-pieced unit from step 1 in half widthwise, wrong sides together; finger-press the ends of the folded edge to make a crease. Fold each unit from step 2 in half, right sides together, bringing the triangles together; finger-press the end of the fold closest to the triangles to make a crease. Stitch a unit from step 2 to each side of the long string-pieced unit from step 1 as shown, matching the creases. Stitch with the shorter unit on top. Make 12.

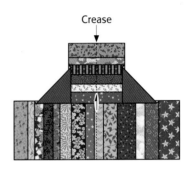

Crease

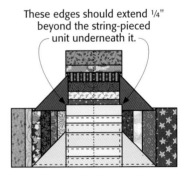

These edges should extend ¼" beyond the string-pieced unit underneath it.

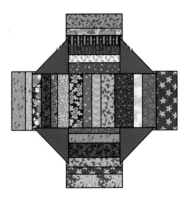

Make 12.

Tip

You may find it is quicker to line up the second short unit with the first and eliminate the finger pressing on half of the short units and one edge of the long unit.

4. Trace 2 of the templates on page 78 onto a piece of template plastic or tracing paper and cut them out. Tape the templates to the underside of the 12½"-square ruler as shown, with the centers overlapping each other.

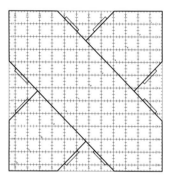

5. Place the ruler over each unit from step 3, lining up the templates with the string-pieced sections. Trim 2 adjacent sides even with the ruler; rotate the unit 180°, realign the ruler, and trim the remaining 2 sides. The blocks should measure 12½" x 12½". Make 12 blocks.

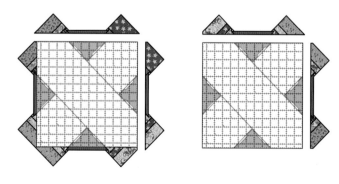

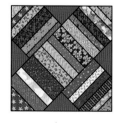

Make 12.

Making the String-Pieced Rail Fence Blocks

1. Referring to "String-Piecing Techniques" on page 11, use the multicolored strips that are at least 5½" long to make 34 string-pieced units that measure at least 5½" wide and 12½" long. Press the seams in one direction. Trim each unit so that it measures exactly 4½" x 12½".

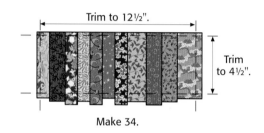

Trim to 12½".

Trim to 4½".

Make 34.

2. Stitch a string-pieced unit from step 1 to each side of a red 4½" x 12½" strip as shown. Press the seams toward the red strips. Make 17 blocks.

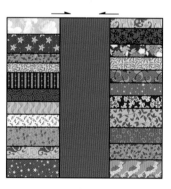

Make 17.

Assembling the Quilt

Refer to "Assembly and Finishing" on pages 16–20.

1. Sew the string-pieced "X" blocks and Rail Fence blocks and the red 12½" squares into rows as shown. Press the seams toward the "X" blocks and red squares. Sew the rows together. Press the seams in the directions indicated.

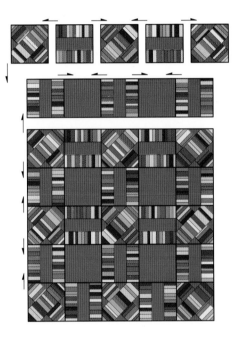

2. Refer to "Borders with Mitered Corners" on page 17 to stitch the red 6½"-wide strips to the quilt.

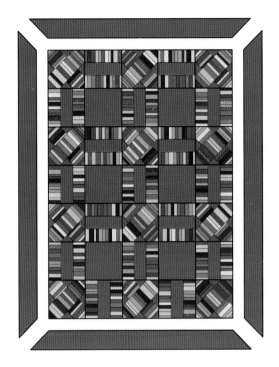

3. Layer the quilt top with batting and backing; baste. Quilt as desired.

4. Bind the edges of the quilt.

Tip

*The large, plain blocks
are great places to showcase some
special quilting.*

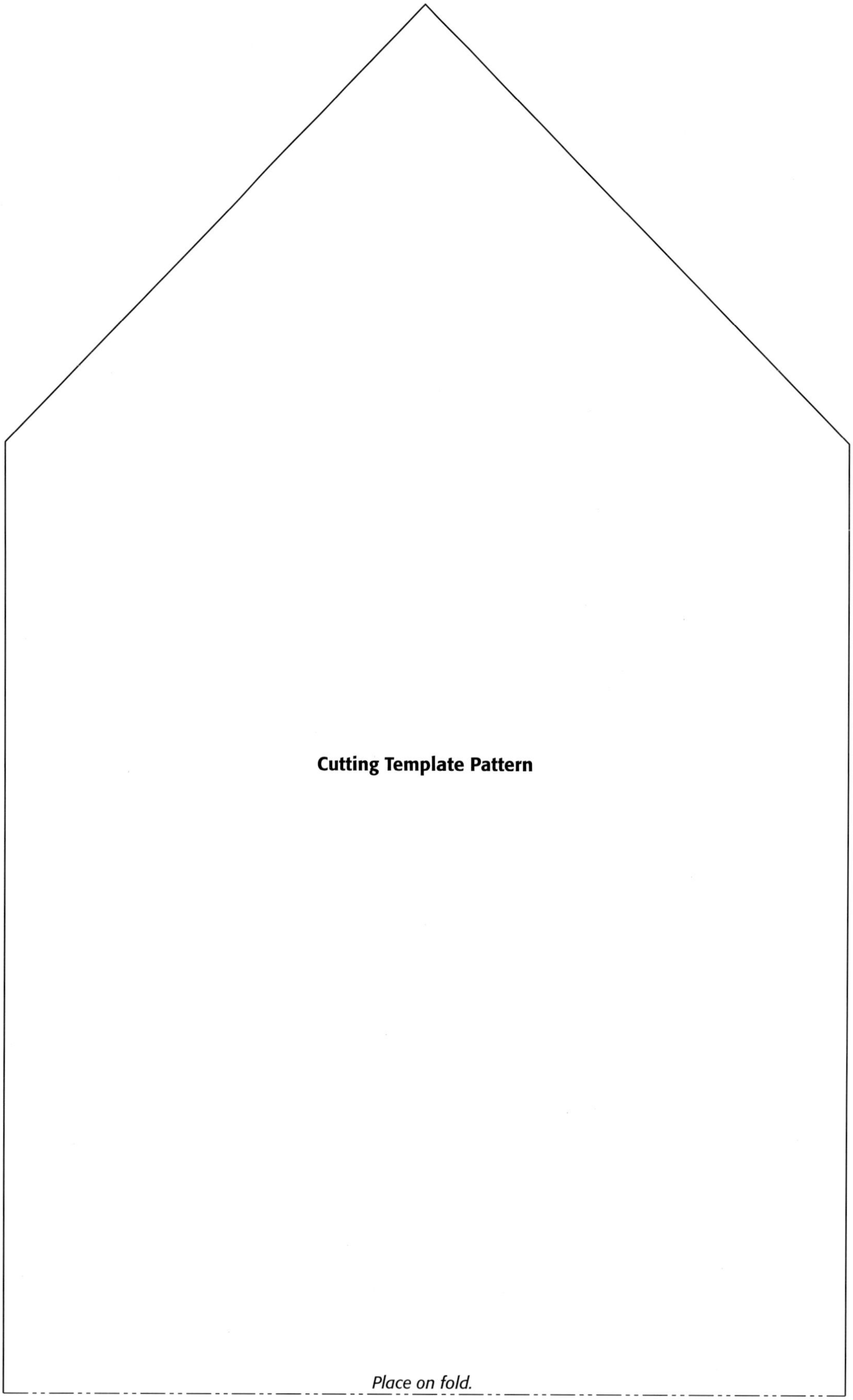

Cutting Template Pattern

Place on fold.

Stars of Freedom

Finished quilt size: 57½" x 79½" ~ Finished block size: 6⅝" equilateral triangle

Dig out your red and blue scraps for this fun quilt.
Although it may look complicated, it is simply triangles put together into rows.
Careful placement of the blue and red triangles forms the stars.
What a great way to show your patriotism!

Materials

Yardage is based on 42"-wide fabric.

2⅞ yds. *total* of assorted red scraps *or* 12 fat quarters for triangles

2⅞ yds. *total* of assorted blue scraps *or* 12 fat quarters for triangles

2⅞ yds. light-colored fabric for background

5¼ yds. fabric for backing

⅝ yd. fabric for straight-grain binding *or* 1 yd. for bias binding

65" x 87" piece of batting

Cutting

From the assorted red scraps or fat quarters, cut:

Approximately 119 strips that vary in width from 1" to 2½" and are at least 18" long. Strips that are less than 18" long but at least 10" long also will work, but you will need twice as many strips (refer to "String-Piecing Techniques" on page 11 for piecing and cutting instructions).

From the assorted blue scraps or fat quarters, cut:

Approximately 119 strips that vary in width from 1" to 2½" and are at least 18" long. Strips that are less than 18" long but at least 10" long also will work, but you will need twice as many strips (refer to "String-Piecing Techniques" on page 11 for piecing and cutting instructions).

From the light-colored fabric, cut:
14 strips, 6½" x 42"

From the binding fabric, cut:
7 strips, 2½" x 42", for straight-grain binding or enough 2½"-wide bias strips to measure no less than 282" when pieced together. If you choose to make the quilt with rounded corners as shown on page 79, you must use bias binding.

Making the String-Pieced Triangles

Refer to "String-Pieced Units for 60° Triangles" on page 12.

1. Use the red strips to make 17 string-pieced units that measure at least 6½" wide and 18" long, staggering the strip ends about ½". In the same manner, make 17 blue string-pieced units. Press the seams in one direction. Trim each unit so that it measures exactly 6½" wide.

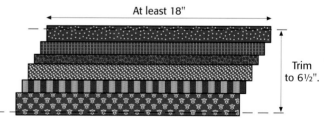

Make 17 red units and 17 blue units.

2. Cut 60° triangles from the blue and red string-pieced units. Each string-pieced unit will yield 4 triangles. Cut 66 blue triangles and 66 red triangles.

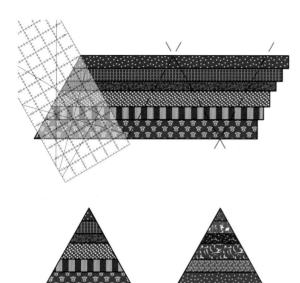

Cut 66 red triangles.   Cut 66 blue triangles.

3. Refer to step 2 to cut the light-colored strips into triangles. Each strip will yield 9 triangles. Cut 118. Mark the bottom of each triangle with a chalk pencil or straight pin so you will know which edge is on the straight of grain. The straight-grain edge will be placed on the quilt outer edges when the triangles are assembled.

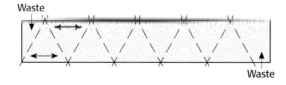

Waste

Waste

Assembling the Quilt

Refer to "Assembly and Finishing" on pages 16–20.

1. Sew the triangles into vertical rows as shown. Make sure the straight-grain edge of the light-colored triangles is parallel to the outer edge of the top. Press the seams in opposite directions from row to row. Sew the rows together. Press the seams in one direction. Trim the top and bottom edges ¼" beyond the tips of the red and blue triangles.

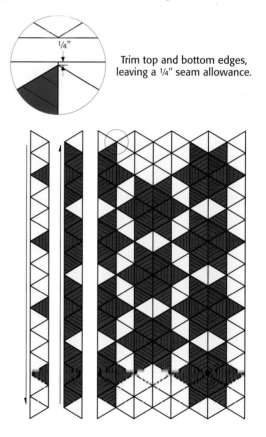

Trim top and bottom edges, leaving a ¼" seam allowance.

2. Layer the quilt top with batting and backing; baste. Quilt as desired.

3. To make the quilt with rounded corners as shown on page 79, trim the corners, using a dinner plate as a guide.

4. Bind the edges of the quilt.

Dazzling Diamonds

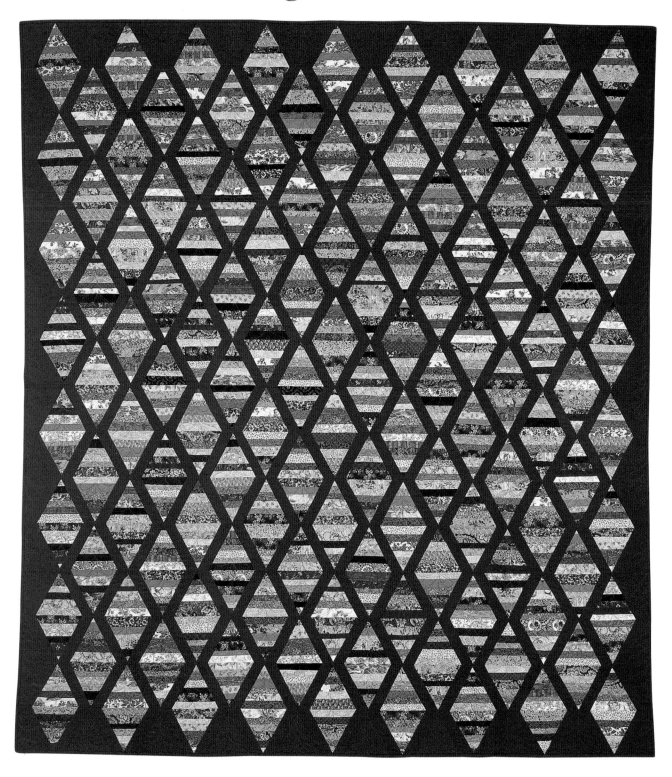

Finished quilt size: 86⅝" x 92"~ Finished block size: 6⅝" equilateral triangle

A group of fat quarters from a fabric collection was the inspiration for this sparkling quilt. I loved all the rich-looking purples and greens in the grouping and chose other fabrics with these colors from my scraps to go with the grouping. When I was finished, I had to really look for the pieces from the collection, since I had added so many other fabrics.

Materials

Yardage is based on 42"-wide fabric.

10⅜ yds. *total* of assorted purple and green scraps *or* 42 fat quarters for triangles

5⅞ yds. raspberry fabric for sashing strips and setting triangles

9 yds. fabric for backing

⅞ yd. fabric for binding

95" x 100" piece of batting

Cutting

From the assorted purple and green scraps or fat quarters, cut:
Approximately 448 strips that vary in width from 1" to 2½" and are at least 18" long. Strips that are less than 18" long but at least 10" long will also work, but you will need twice as many strips (refer to "String-Piecing Techniques" on page 11 for piecing and cutting instructions).

From the raspberry fabric, cut:
29 strips, 6½" x 42"

From the binding fabric, cut:
10 strips, 2½" x 42"

Making the String-Pieced Triangles

Refer to "String-Pieced Units for 60° Triangles" on page 12.

1. Use the purple and green strips to make 64 string-pieced units that measure at least 6½" wide and 18" long, staggering the strip ends about ½". Press the seams in one direction. Trim each unit so that it measures exactly 6½" wide.

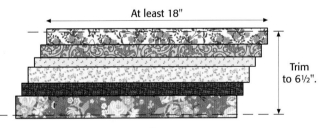

At least 18"

Trim to 6½".

Make 64.

2. Cut 60° triangles from the string-pieced units. Each string-pieced unit will yield 4 triangles. Cut 256 triangles.

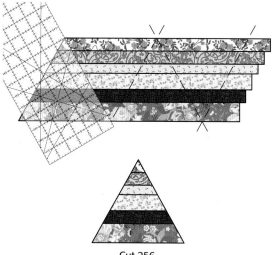

Cut 256.

Making the Setting Triangles and Sashing Strips

1. To make the top and bottom setting triangles, refer to "String-Pieced Units for 60° Triangles" on page 12 to cut 16 triangles from 2 of the raspberry strips. Each strip will yield 9 triangles. Mark the bottom of each triangle with a chalk pencil or straight pin so you will know which edge is on the straight of grain. The straight-grain edge will be placed on the quilt outer edges when the triangles are assembled.

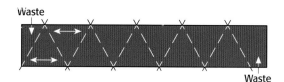

2. To make the side setting triangles, cut 32 half triangles from 3 of the raspberry strips. To make the half triangles, fold the strips in half widthwise. It does not matter if right or wrong sides are together. By folding the strips in half,

you will cut a half triangle and a reverse half triangle at the same time. Make a straight cut along the raw end of each strip. Line up the 60°-angle mark on the ruler with the top of the strip, leaving approximately 1" from the straightened edge at the bottom of the strip as shown. The 1" measurement is approximate because the pieces will be trimmed a little after the quilt is put together. Cut along the right edge of the ruler. This will make the first half triangle and reverse half triangle. Move over about 1" at the top of the strip and make a straight cut. Continue alternating straight and 60°-angle cuts along the length of each strip. Each strip will yield 6 half triangles and 6 reverse half triangles.

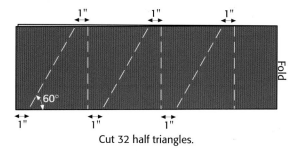

Cut 32 half triangles.

3. From the remaining 24 raspberry strips, cut 288 sashing strips. To cut the strips, fold each strip in half widthwise. It does not matter if right or wrong sides are together. By folding the strips in half, you will cut a sashing strip and reverse sashing strip at the same time. Line up the 60°-angle mark on the ruler with the top of each strip at the raw end. Cut along the right edge of the ruler. Make 2"-wide cuts along the length of each strip, parallel to the first 60° cut. Each strip will yield 6 sashing strips and 6 reverse sashing strips.

Cut 288 sashing strips.

Assembling the Quilt

Refer to "Assembly and Finishing" on pages 16–20.

1. Join the string-pieced triangles, the setting triangles, and the sashing strips into rows as shown. Begin and end each row with a side setting triangle. Use the top and bottom setting triangles in the top and bottom rows only. Press the seams toward the sashing strips. Sew the rows together. Press the seams in one direction.

2. Trim the sides of the quilt ¼" beyond the point where the sashing strips meet.

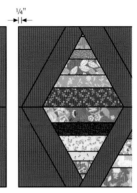

Trim ¼" beyond sashing.

3. Layer the quilt top with batting and backing; baste. Quilt as desired.

4. Bind the edges of the quilt.

Tip

You will be sewing the triangles and sashing strips together along the bias edges. The pieces will ease together very nicely. Just be careful not to stretch them. Note that as you sew a triangle piece to a sashing piece, the tip of the triangle will be about ¼" down from the tip of the sashing. This will seem strange, but it will make the diamonds seem to float on the background. The tips of the diamonds won't touch each other and there will not be the bulk you would normally find when so many seams come together in one spot. When you sew a sashing piece to a triangle, these pieces will line up as they normally do.

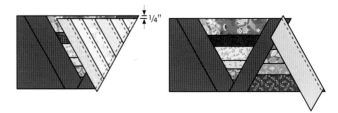

Finished quilt size: 64" x 83" ~ Finished block size: 6½" x 6½"

This color-washed beauty is a great way to use up lots of scraps.
Just separate a wide variety of blue, green, and purple fabrics into light,
medium, and dark stacks, and you're ready to go.
Beautiful machine quilting by Jeannie Brewster in metallic threads
makes this quilt really sparkle.

Materials

Yardage is based on 42"-wide fabric.

5⅛ yds. *total* of assorted dark blue, dark green, and dark purple scraps *or* 21 fat quarters for blocks and setting triangles

5 yds. *total* of assorted medium blue, medium green, and medium purple scraps *or* 20 fat quarters for blocks and setting triangles

1¾ yds. *total* of assorted light blue, light green, and light purple scraps *or* 8 fat quarters for blocks and setting triangles

5¾ yds. fabric for backing

¾ yd. fabric for binding

72" x 91" piece of batting

Tip

Pick fabrics that read as light, medium, or dark. Fabrics that are both dark and light will be distracting. Anything goes as long as the color fits in; this is a great quilt for using up lots of scraps.

Cutting

From the light scraps or fat quarters, cut:
Approximately 136 strips that vary in width from 1" to 2½" and are at least 8½" long. Strips that are at least 16" long will make 2 units, and you will need only half the amount of strips (refer to "String-Piecing Techniques" on page 11 for piecing and cutting instructions).

From the medium scraps or fat quarters, cut:
Approximately 432 strips that vary in width from 1" to 2½" and are at least 8½" long. Strips that are at least 16" long will make 2 units, and you will need only half the amount of strips (refer to "String-Piecing Techniques" on page 11 for piecing and cutting instructions).

From the dark scraps or fat quarters, cut:
Approximately 430 strips that vary in width from 1" to 2½" and are at least 8½" long. Strips that are at least 16" long will make 2 units, and you will need only half the amount of strips (refer to "String-Piecing Techniques" on page 11 for piecing and cutting instructions).

Approximately 10 strips that vary in width from 1" to 2½" and are at least 9½" long. Strips that are at least 18" long will make 2 units, and you will need only half the amount of strips (refer to "String-Piecing Techniques" on page 11 for piecing and cutting instructions).

From the binding fabric, cut:
8 strips, 2½" x 42"

Making the String-Pieced Blocks

1. Referring to "String-Piecing Techniques" on page 11, use the light, medium, and dark strips that are at least 8½" long to make string-pieced units that are at least 7½" wide . Make 12 units with all light-colored strips, 12 units with a mixture of light-colored and medium-colored strips, 36 units with all medium-colored strips, 24 units with a mixture of medium-colored and dark-colored strips, and 28 units with all dark-colored strips. Press the seams in one direction. Trim each unit so that it measures exactly 7½" x 7½".

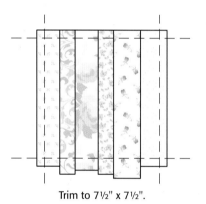

Trim to 7½" x 7½".

Make 12 light.

Make 12 light/medium.

Make 36 medium.

Make 24 medium/dark.

Make 28 dark.

2. To make the string-pieced units for the setting triangles, use the remaining dark strips that are at least 8½" long to make 14 string-pieced units that are at least 8" wide. Press the seams in one direction. Trim 8 of these units so they measure exactly 7½" x 7½"; trim the remaining 6 units so they measure exactly 8" x 8". Using the dark strips that are at least 9½" long, make 1 string-pieced unit that is at least 9" wide. Press the seams in one direction. Trim the unit so it measures exactly 9" x 9". Keep these units separate from the step 1 units.

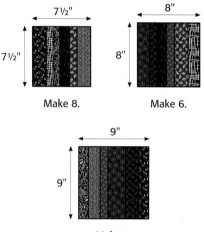

Make 8.

Make 6.

Make 1.

3. Draw a diagonal line on the wrong side of 6 light, 6 light/medium, 18 medium, 12 medium/dark, and 14 dark units from step 1 as shown. Place each marked unit right sides together with an unmarked unit; stitch ¼" from both sides of the marked line. Cut on the

marked line. Press the seams open. Trim the squares so they measure exactly 7" x 7". You should have 12 light, 12 light/medium, 36 medium, 24 medium/dark, and 28 dark blocks.

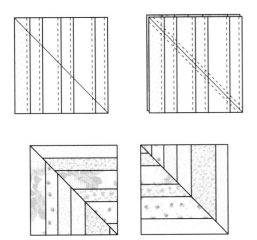

Trim to 7" x 7".
Make 12 light, 12 light/medium,
36 medium, 24 medium/dark, and 28 dark.

4. To make the setting triangles for the top and bottom edges of the quilt, use the 8" x 8" dark units from step 2 to make 6 dark blocks as shown in step 3. Do not trim the blocks. Cut them in half as shown. Keep the top triangles separate from the bottom triangles; they are different.

Top triangles

Bottom triangles

5. Cut 4 of the 7½" x 7½" dark units from step 2 in half diagonally as shown for the left-edge setting triangles; cut the remaining 4 units in half diagonally in the opposite direction for the right-edge setting triangles. Note that these units are not sewn together as the previous units have been; they are simply cut in half.

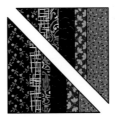

Left edge triangles   Right edge triangles

6. To make the corner setting triangles, cut the 9" x 9" dark unit made in step 2 in half twice diagonally as shown.

Bottom

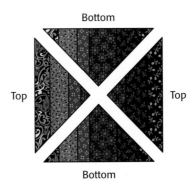

Top   Top

Bottom

Tip

It will be helpful to keep these triangles separated in plastic bags and label them: top, bottom, left side, right side, top corners, and bottom corners.

Assembling the Quilt

Refer to "Assembly and Finishing" on pages 16–20.

1. Sew the blocks and setting triangles into diagonal rows as shown, carefully following the illustration for block placement. The setting triangles are oversized and will be trimmed later. Press the seams in opposite directions from row to row. Sew the rows together. Press the seams in one direction. Refer to "Assembling Diagonally Set Quilts" on page 16 to trim the quilt edges.

2. Layer the quilt top with batting and backing; baste. Quilt as desired.

3. Bind the edges of the quilt.

Rainy Day Blues

Finished quilt size: 84" x 98"~ Finished block size: 7" x 7"

*We have lots of rainy days in western Washington where I live,
and I love spending those days quilting. A large variety of blue fabrics give
depth and interest to this Drunkard's Path block.
This is a great quilt for learning to work with curved seams.*

Materials

Yardage is based on 42"-wide fabric.

5⅞ yds. light-colored fabric for blocks

4½ yds. *total* of assorted blue scraps *or* 18 fat quarters for blocks

8⅝ yds. fabric for backing

⅞ yd. fabric for binding

92" x 106" piece of batting

Frosted template plastic or freezer paper

Cutting

From the assorted blue scraps or fat quarters, cut:

Approximately 864 strips that vary in width from 1" to 2½" and are at least 7½" long. Strips that are at least 14" long will make 2 units, and strips at least 20½" long will make 3 units. You will need fewer strips if you use strips longer than 7½" (refer to "String-Piecing Techniques" on page 11 for piecing and cutting instructions).

From the light-colored fabric, cut:
15 strips, 10" x 42"

5 strips, 7½" x 42"; crosscut the strips into 24 squares, 7½" x 7½"

From the binding fabric, cut:
10 strips, 2½" x 42"

Tip

*Don't try to do all of the cutting at once.
This can be tedious and tiring. I like to cut a
variety of strips and then start sewing.
By alternating the tasks often, you'll be able to
stick with the job longer and your quilt
will be done before you know it.*

Making the String-Pieced Drunkard's Path Blocks

1. Referring to "String-Piecing Techniques" on page 11, use the assorted blue strips to make 44 string-pieced units that are at least 7½" wide and 20" long. Press the seams in one direction. Trim each unit so that it measures exactly 6½" wide.

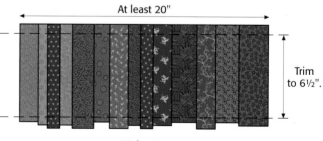

At least 20"

Trim to 6½".

Make 44.

2. Sew several 6½"-wide sections together end to end to make one long unit. Just sew together a few at a time. You will cut out pieces from this unit for the Drunkard's Path block. As you get close to the end of the unit, sew some more 6½" sections onto it, and continue cutting.

3. Trace the Drunkard's Path templates on page 95 onto template plastic or the dull side of freezer paper. The ¼" seam allowance is already included.

4. Using the fan-shaped template, trace around the template on the right side of the string-pieced unit as shown. Line up the grain-line arrow on the template with the strips to make sure you are straight. Cut out the pieces on the traced lines. If you are using freezer paper, iron the shiny side to your fabric. The freezer paper will adhere to the fabric, and you can cut around the template without having to trace around it. Then, pull the freezer paper off and reuse it. It can be reused many times before it will quit sticking. Cut 144 fan-shaped units.

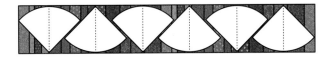

5. Using the concave-shaped template, cut 144 pieces from the light-colored 10" x 42" strips as shown.

6. Fold each concave piece in half, wrong sides together, bringing the short ends together; finger-press the fold at the curved edge to make a crease. Fold each fan-shaped unit in half, right sides together, bringing the straight edges together; finger-press the fold at the curved edge to make a crease.

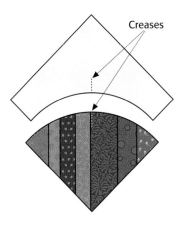

Creases

7. Pin each concave piece to a fan-shaped piece, placing the concave piece on top as shown and matching creases. The top crease will sink into the bottom crease, and the pieces will stay together much easier while being sewn. Place pins at the crease and at each end, then pin several places in between, easing the 2 fabrics to fit. The more you pin, the less likely you will have puckers. Carefully stitch these 2 pieces together, removing the pins as you come to them. Press the seam towards the concave piece. This is such a gentle curve that no clipping is necessary. Make 144 string-pieced Drunkard's Path blocks.

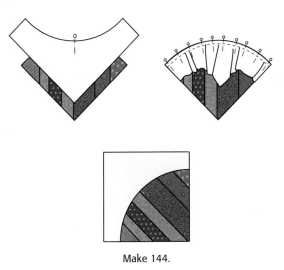

Make 144.

Assembling the Quilt

Refer to "Assembly and Finishing" on pages 16–20.

1. Join the string-pieced Drunkard's Path blocks and 24 light-colored 7½" squares into rows as shown. Press the seams in opposite directions from row to row. Sew the rows together. Press the seams in one direction.

2. Layer the quilt top with batting and backing; baste. Quilt as desired.

3. Bind the edges of the quilt. If you wish to make a scrappy binding as shown, cut 2½"-wide strips of blue scraps in varying lengths. Sew these together to achieve the total length required to go around the quilt, and then bind the quilt as usual.

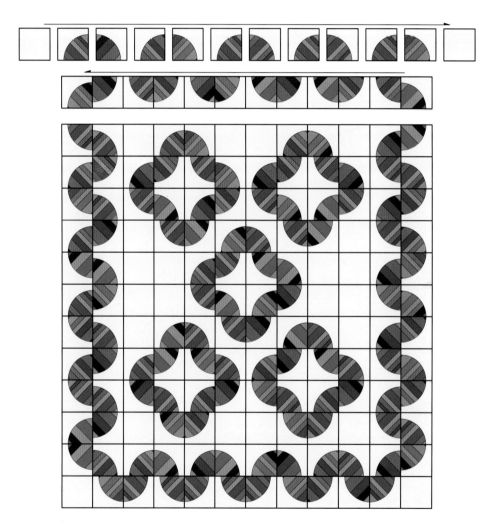

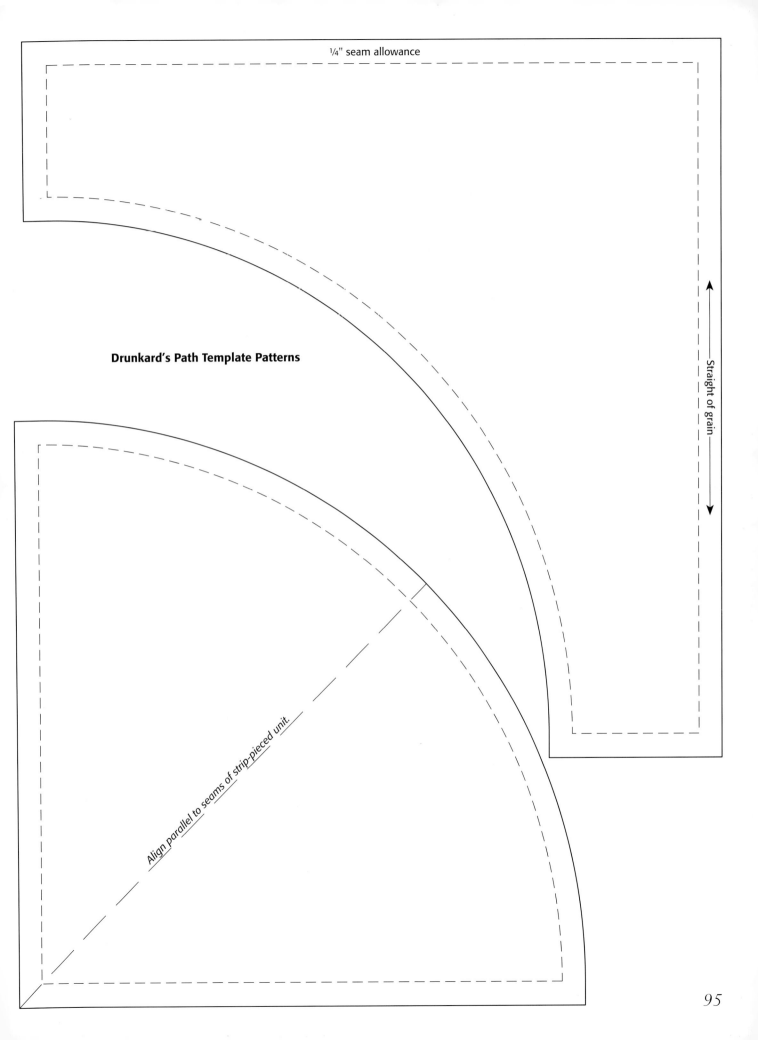

¼" seam allowance

Straight of grain

Drunkard's Path Template Patterns

Align parallel to seams of strip-pieced unit.

¼" seam allowance

95

About the Author

Evelyn Sloppy lives with her husband, Dean, on eighty wooded acres in western Washington, where she savors the peaceful country life and visits from their four children and four grandchildren. She has quilted since 1991 and has enjoyed designing her own quilts and teaching at several area quilt shops since 1998. Her quilting interests are broad, but she especially enjoys making scrappy, traditional quilts. This is Evelyn's third book with Martingale & Company. Her first book was *Log Cabin Fever*, followed by *Frayed-Edge Fun*, both published in 2002.